MAKING THE MOST FUTURE-FIT ORGANISATION

TRANSFORMING ORGANISATION TO THRIVE IN THE VUCCAD BUSINESS LANDSCAPE.

DR. AMIT DAS

Copyright © Dr. Amit Das
All Rights Reserved.

To

All my bosses and mentors who made a difference in my professional career.

"Transformation is not without danger, but adopting agility may mitigate this by giving organisations the resilience they need to deal with constant change. An adaptive organisation is one that not only survives, but also flourishes in the long run, surviving the test of time."

– Dr. Amit Das, Motivational Speaker, Leadership Coach and Mentor.

Contents

Foreword — vii

Preface — xiii

Acknowledgements — xxi

1. Distinctive Features Of The Future-fit Organisation — 1

2. Reshaping The Future Of Work Experience — 50

3. Solving The Adaptable Leadership Paradox For Long-term — 96

References — 145

About The Author — 149

Foreword

FOREWARD

"The measure of intelligence is the ability to change."-Albert Einstein

Dear Readers,

Thank you for taking the time to learn more about the secrets of making the most future-fit organisation . The author recognises that intelligent, motivated individuals like you have special gifts to give the world, but it's difficult to do in this VUCCAD business environment. The author has spent his entire professional career assisting managers in increasing their productivity, which he describes as the capacity to make progress on the results that matter most to them.

Regardless of the audience or venue, reading this book puts the reader on a unique and advantageous platform to connect in a more intelligent and successful manner. This book is well-researched and educational for people of all ages and genders. This book, "Making The Most Future-Fit Organisation" is a quest to perceive even the most mundane things in a new light. Its goal is to assist you to harness your capacity to become more adaptive and use it to your advantage in order to rise above the mediocre tides in all aspects of your life. It reveals numerous methods for intentionally cultivating a mindset that refuses to be superficial about life.

"There is no exact formula for predicting the future of any industry; nonetheless, business executives can envision the next day based on the unique qualities of each organisation."

The contents of this book will provide a deep reservoir of ideas and techniques for producing remarkable outcomes, competitive advantages, and long-term results for leaders, consultants, and organisational advisors. This book aims to teach you how critical it is to be adaptive every day toward achieving the things that matter most to you, leaving no stone unturned, and to develop a mindset of seeing the most overlooked aspects of life not only for what they are or appear to be, but also for what they could be.

This book outlines the importance of adaptive leadership in an organisation, clearing your head of clutter, and sticking to a single-point agenda. The days of traditional, stability-oriented organisations are numbered. Organisations built for both stability and dynamism with networks of teams and people-centered cultures governed by common goals and co-created value for all stakeholders are replacing them.

To survive and prosper, an organisation must be able to foresee, plan for, respond to, and adapt to problems and opportunities. It goes beyond risk management to take a more comprehensive view of a company's health and performance.

> *"An adaptive organisation is one that not only survives, but also flourishes in the long run, surviving the test of time."*

Every company relies on its leadership to strengthen, organise, and shift resources in order to make the most efficient and effective use of them in order to enhance returns on investment and develop adaptiveness.

Dr. Amit Das provides a step-by-step approach in this book on how to create an excellent adaptive culture at your organisation. The author demonstrates how to uncover your hidden culture, transform ideals into actions, and open up communication across layers. To keep your culture thriving for the long term, the author emphasises the significance of being clear from the top, building trust, and providing support structures. As Dr. Amit Das demonstrates in his book, by building your culture, you can increase communication, raise morale, encourage trust, and keep negativity at bay within your team. The author provides businesses with a step-by-step strategy for analysing, creating, and implementing iterative adaptive cultural transformation, with each success building on prior achievements. As a result, the company continues to adapt in ways that reduce stress, encourage learning, and promote organisational wellness.

Indeed, it may have increased as businesses realise their present systems are incapable of keeping up with the current rate of change. Consider whether your processes are flexible enough. Could your essential business systems adapt quickly to significant operational changes? Organisations with inbuilt adaptability skills are more likely than others to have responded quickly to the recent epidemic. Dr. Amit Das has interviewed hundreds of the most prolific performers to learn the best strategies for pursuing and maintaining organisational greatness. He discovered a pattern of unusual actions that distinguished these exceptional people.

"Transformation is not without danger, but adopting agility may mitigate this by giving organisations the resilience they need to deal with constant change."

The book, "Making The Most Future-Fit Organisation" delves into how and where these efforts must be made in order for this to happen. The book is the result of the author's own endeavor to improve organisational performance. The most current concepts, as well as new observations and opinions, have been chosen and assembled. It will be extremely beneficial to the readers in their pursuit of perfection.

> *"During these times of upheaval and uncertainty, many organisations recognise the need for speed. Leaders perceive an opportunity to accelerate their organisations' pace by doing even more in the areas mentioned above in the future."*

Respondents most typically cite more efficient decision making, clearer communication, and the use of technology to better engage consumers and staff when asked about the key chances to attain higher speed. The author offers the most effective tactics and step-by-step instructions for you to construct your own particular road to excellence in this book. You'll also find better methods to collaborate with colleagues, respond more effectively to coaching and mentoring, and become more positive and self-directed in your thoughts and actions, resulting in more personal and professional pleasure.

This book attempts to provide insights into the many pathways, courses, and drives that world-class enterprises have constructed in order to achieve the pinnacles of greatness. This book provides cutting-edge material, including innovative and unusual study aids as well as fresh, thought-provoking content, with an emphasis on integrating corporate agility, or adaptiveness, into practical management.

This book, "Making The Most Future-Fit Organisation" draws on first-hand experience from high-performance operations to deliver vital adaptive leadership lessons as well as clear, accessible, and practical insights on managing teams in any corporate setting. This book provides a new and fascinating viewpoint on the factors that influence team and organisational greatness. Dr. Amit Das, the book's author, has a unique combination of expertise and insight, having worked as a management consultant. His insights and interviews from business sectors are used to demonstrate the obstacles to high performance and leadership.

The materials include a performance model that can be applied to a wide range of organisations, focusing on people's attitudes rather than skills; a process for closing the gap between desired and actual outcomes; how to accelerate performance in real time; exhibiting a set of behaviours that the capacity of an organisation to function efficiently, adapt properly, adjust correctly, and grow from within is referred to as organisational health. Take a path that leads to significant performance increases and a great culture where everyone is prepared to succeed with this leadership.

> *"Just like strategy, writing a book takes deep contemplation to narrate a theory in a very lucid manner. Hence, the author could establish his thought process for readers."*

The book questions a lot of conventional thinking from the past, but it is harsh when marketing hype prevails over actual knowledge. In the process, it provides a different route that is theoretically complete, provokes thought, and aids in the implementation of sensible judgments.

> *"A significant gap exists between corporate strategy and what really succeeds in the marketplace as a result of the disruption caused by data and technology over the past two decades."*

Numerous new models, such as holacracy, networked organisations, and agile organisations, to mention a few, have developed, but leaders must understand which ones are most effective. How do you create an organisation that can adapt to markets that change quickly? What sort of organisation—and how would you run it—delivers both speed and scale?

Additionally, it will encourage readers to remember their most outstanding leaders, enjoy the richness of their own life experiences, and keep pursuing chances to become a better adaptive leader for their organisation.

Get your copy today to get started on your adaptive journey!

So, happy reading and learning to all my readers.

Carpe diem.

Dr. Amit Das

Motivational Speaker, Leadership Coach, and Mentor.

Preface

Today, more than half of the world's population is under thirty years of age. The Internet has now been a part of two generations' lives. It doesn't take an anthropology degree to see that the world has changed significantly during the past 25 years.

In business, change is the only constant, although it is rarely as unexpected or as overpowering as it has been in 2022. The coronavirus pandemic has supended a number of industries, from hospitality to energy, that appeared positioned for success in the new decade until lately. Businesses are now scrambling to pick up the debris while navigating an uncertain future. Under normal conditions, change management is a difficult task. However, when COVID-19 was taken into account, organisational transformation takes on a whole new meaning.

Your life may improve by accident, but your initiatives will not. With me, you can start managing your organisation more effectively.

What exactly is adaptability?

Being adaptable means being flexible. Accepting change is the definition of adaptability. While agility or adaptability has always been crucial in the modern workplace, it is now more important than ever. In this unique situation, businesses that adapt quickly and establish a new normal are more likely to prosper.

Organisations do not adapt quickly enough to keep up with changing requirements, and governance and management methods do not generate the required results. The development of a good organisational performance system can help to solve these issues. We frequently ignore this extremely crucial truth, "transformation to thrive," at our peril. An emergent living organisation will lack the cohesion to function successfully and will quickly turn to the old ego-crutches of control-based management.

What happens if you put pressure on a crystal glass?

It usually becomes weaker over time and finally breaks. Crystal glasses, like many other items and living things, are delicate. What is the polar opposite of delicate? Strong, tenacious, and adaptable come to mind. Being robust, resilient, and flexible, on the other hand, is not the polar opposite of being fragile. It is *"adaptable" or "agile."* When you push on it, it not only bounces back but it bounces harder. It's almost as if it's a muscle. It expands as you stretch it or apply power to it. Larger, more established organisations can also be adaptable.

The fact is clear: some businesses will position themselves to swiftly adapt to the ever-increasing rate of change, while others will become obsolete and finally cease to exist. While the likelihood of businesses dying has grown with time, the true picture of the impact of rapid change on organisations is more complex. If companies want to know how to effectively respond to these issues, they must not only think about the correct change management theories, procedures, and strategies, but they must also think about mindset and behavior transformation, since that is the true difficulty.

What VUCCAD stands for?

- **Volatility:** Volatility, in a broad sense, is frequently associated with either market volatility—quick swings and changes in company market capitalisation, frequently during swings from bull to bear markets—or volatile personalities—people prone to wild behavioural swings.

- **Uncertainty:** While it's crucial to have preparations in place to get through these crises, forward-thinking companies are also prepared to use these moments as chances to strengthen their market position and competitiveness by taking advantage of uncertainty to their advantage. The only real certainty in business settings is, well, business uncertainty.
- **Complexity:** Complexity in business receives negative press. That is not unexpected. Complexity has important advantages over its more obvious drawbacks, particularly in dynamic and unpredictable contexts.
- **Conflict:** Workplace disagreements are all too prevalent in the commercial world. Think about the following examples of real-life conflicts. The lack of an integrated framework for handling business conflicts results in low morale and high turnover in many organisations. Rapid action in times of conflict can significantly cut down on the expense and duration of dispute settlement.
- **Ambiguity:** Ambiguity in the workplace is a complicated issue. Occasionally, ambiguity can be advantageous, but more often than not, the absence of direction and clarity stifles activity and prevents successful outcomes.
- **Dynamism:** We can better feel and react to dynamics at play across an organisation that functions as a living organism if we develop into more natural and conscious leaders. The rates at which new enterprises join the market, expand, and depart the market are used to gauge business dynamism, a crucial component of the

expansion of the economy.

Organisations that learn and adapt to problems in a volatile, unpredictable, complex, conflicting, ambiguous, and dynamic (VUCCAD) business environment have a significant competitive edge. Leaders must adjust as well, frequently making significant changes because their roles might be procedural and rule-driven. Leaders must be adaptable and sensitive to the fast-changing world in order to flourish in this (VUCCAD) environment. This begins with paying attention to critical input that will lead you to the result you aim to achieve via your organisational efforts. It is your responsibility as a systems leader to build an organisation that can adapt to the difficulties it confronts on a daily basis.

Systems thinking entails attempting to comprehend the systems that surround you. To do more than just respond to circumstances as they occur. Instead, consider how the world truly works. In today's fast-changing competitive (VUCCAD) world, merely pursuing efficiency would not be enough. So I will show you a framework for establishing adaptable organisation that are quick and agile in responding to market changes.

Your mission is to build an organisation that learns how to adapt and survive. To do this, you must promote organisational learning aimed at increasing your capability to meet organisational goals. Leaders must also realize that organisational results are not something that can be generated directly, but rather indirectly, through instilling a set of simple norms that govern each group member's work. To develop system-level behavior, you must concentrate on the underlying rules that generate it. The issue is that CEOs, administrators, and other organisational leaders are always striving to get more out of their teams and organisations in order to improve both internal efficiency and outward influence. They want to work smarter and leave a bigger impression on the world faster.

> *"The issue is that humans do not act like a collection of gears. Their intentions are often mixed, and you're all aware that they may participate in more subtle types of resistance, which gears do not."*

Everything is available at the press of a button in today's competitive world, and life is fast and seamless, with an internet highway running parallel to us. Connecting via virtual setup has become a necessary element of our lives. This, paired with the impending danger of COVID-19, has made working from home and on internet platforms the new normal. The hybrid office is more popular than ever. A hybrid workplace is one in which some workers work from the office while others work from home. This gives you greater control over when and where you finish your job. Even after COVID, companies like Google have stated that they will continue to use hybrid mode. Similar moves have been contemplated by several other corporations, including Microsoft, Twitter, and Verizon. Unfortunately, employees in India are struggling to cope with the heavy demand.

Burnout among employees is on the rise. Employee happiness and productivity are inextricably linked. Many corporate executives were terrified of flexible work environments before the COVID-19 epidemic. Just a few weeks ago, the prospect of all workers working from home for weeks or months would have prompted panic attacks. There will be extra challenges for teams to be able to problem solve effectively, develop strong solutions and execute them across the business and activities in a timely and efficient fashion.

You don't get to choose whether or not your organisation is a complex adaptive system since it is made up of individuals interacting socially and with their surroundings. However, you have the option of embracing this reality and using it to your benefit. All companies have the potential to be learning organisations. This is due to their capability to gather and respond to input from the real world, such as consumer data, market forces, and competition. The majority of organisational challenges you confront are caused by gaps between how organisations actually operate and how you believe they work. As a result of feedback, these things get more aligned. It is the leader's responsibility to foster a culture that values and changes in response to input.

In this book, I'll offer some statistics on why and how adaptability is a critical component of leadership, regardless of the team or organisation with which you're working. In addition, you'll discover some of my finest ideas and methods for being an adaptive leader in a fast-paced sector. Most significantly, flexibility is changing to suit new conditions and obstacles, which will ensure your company's or organization's success.

Why is it vital for a leader to be adaptable?

Change is unavoidable. Everything grows and evolves into something better, including the workplace dynamic, corporate strategy, and technological advancements. Adapting and responding is the only way to survive as a leader and face the complexity of change, whether you like it or not. Failure must be considered a chance to learn. To compete, people must be encouraged to try and retest their ideas, as well as given room to iterate. This is adaptation, and adaptable organisations are the result of adaptive leadership.

Are you a leader who can adapt?

Because the world is changing at a breakneck pace, leaders come in a variety of sizes and forms. If you've been keeping up with the newest leadership trends, you've definitely already heard about several techniques and ideals that have proven successful for many current and prospective business leaders. To be honest, there is no right or wrong way to lead, as long as you have the best interests of your team and your organisation at heart. But what if your squad isn't going to stay the same for long? It will shift. And it's not only your team that will alter; it's your workplace culture, your market, everything. This is when you put one of your essential leadership characteristics, namely adaptability, to the test.

"Moving away from a reductive approach that compartmentalises an organisation into silos, hierarchies, and predictable linear linkages is part of this transition in leadership and organisational growth. A worldview characterised by extreme competitiveness, scarcity, fear, and control has been produced by this mentality."- Dr. Amit Das

Acknowledgements

At the outset, I will thank my family for supporting me throughout the journey of writing my book and encouraging me to live my dreams; my son has always been instrumental in giving his inspiration to complete the writing of this book. Despite the fact that I am listed as the author of this book, "Making The Most Future-Fit Organisation" would not have been published if I had depended entirely on my own talents. Creating this book required more than anything—it took a family of dedicated and caring people who were always prepared to lend a hand.

Writing a book while working full-time is no simple task, so I'd want to express my gratitude to my amazing coworkers who act as cheerleaders in equal measure. Thank you, too, to my students and clients for your patience and unflinching support while I worked on this book!

Thank you to everyone who has listened to me argue for doing everything you can to make your life, including your work life, more progressive. I appreciate everyone's assistance throughout the process. This book would not have been possible without each of you having had an impact on my life in some manner.

Lastly, I would like to thank all the people with whom I have been associated. You gave me power. I would like to thank Notion Press for publishing my book. Finally, thank you all for gifting your time to read this book.

I'd want to convey my heartfelt appreciation to the almighty God for bestowing his blessings and being so gracious.

Distinctive Features Of The Future-Fit Organisation

"It is not the strongest of the species that survives, nor the most intelligent. It is the one that is most adaptable to change. "
- Charles Darwin

Organisations are always changing. They are relational and intentional systems made up of clumsy, erratic human interactions that occur inside a convoluted web of stakeholders and people. Organisations are by definition non-linear, and they inherently resemble living systems more than the conventional form that was imposed on them. Organisations and enterprises adapt to ongoing change, gain knowledge, grow, and prosper in the face of constant change.

"Those who know where they belong have the future at their fingertips."

In today's business environment, organisations that see themselves as part of an ecosystem compete better. They have more visibility into their consumers' demands and behaviors when they use external communities, partnerships, and alliances.

- Adaptable organisations are able to identify changes in the external environment rapidly and adapt accordingly.
- Adaptive work frequently entails challenging an organisation's underlying assumptions, challenging the status quo, and implementing changes that may appear harsh but are required.
- Adaptive capacity refers to a person's ability to cope with change and challenges to the status quo. It also includes how a person responds to situational circumstances with suitable actions rather than default inclinations and behaviors.

When company executives recognise that the circumstances are in charge, they may choose actions that boost their adaptability. As a result, leadership becomes more adaptable. Because the future is fundamentally unpredictable, adaptable leadership is essential for long-term success. COVID-19 leaders who could adjust to unpredictability were differentiated from those who couldn't.

> "*Future business practises for any organisations will be founded on living systems logic and will be resilient, adaptable, systems-based, and life-supporting.*"

The world you've known has altered dramatically in only a few years. But, despite this trying moment, keep in mind that generations before you suffered similar difficulties. Your forefathers and mothers, like you, were strong, kind, and determined. The COVID-19 outbreak was quite transitory. You've come out the other side stronger and wiser. COVID-19 has caused widespread alarm for companies and communities all around the world, unlike anything you've ever seen before. The epidemic has brought attention to the need for businesses to be adaptive, but business executives have long recognised this requirement. They had to deal with various problems even before the chaos of 2020.

Most corporate executives believe they have been in a perpetual state of "transformation" for the past two decades, and many are weary of hearing the phrase. It is still doing so. Many industries have been affected. Leaders must set their own interests aside in any tough scenario and devote their resources and efforts to the greater good.

> *"True leaders are visionaries. They are visionaries who encourage creativity and innovation. They provide comfort."*

The COVID-19 issue compelled enterprises all around the world to rethink many elements of their jobs, workforce, and workplace, while also introducing new dangers and opportunities. New business start-ups nearly quadrupled from pre-pandemic levels. Larger companies also went through an "unfreezing" period in which the status quo of how things were done was challenged.

"The pandemic not only interrupted people's lives, but it also provided an opportunity for companies to rethink who they are and where they want to go."

In these exceptional times, businesses have faced unexpected problems and have been attempting to adapt to new methods of working. While businesses strive to minimise the impact on their operations, it is unavoidable that the pandemic has influenced many businesses' future organisational management strategies. The pandemic has heightened the trend of employers taking a greater interest in their employees' financial, physical, and mental health. Some organisations helped the community by moving operations to produce items or provide services to aid in the fight against the epidemic, as well as donating community relief funds and free community services.

- Organisations must take advantage of this potential to turn uncertainty into opportunity throughout their work, workforce, and workplace.
- Organisations should close the loop by supporting their workers' needs after redesigning the job to be done and putting people first.
- Employers must have a clear vision for their working paradigm, whether hybrid, in-person, or remote. However, clarity alone isn't enough. Employees want greater freedom after a live remote work experience, and many will need a good reason to return to in-person work.
- Organisations that solve these issues get a better employee experience, higher loyalty, and more access to talent pools. The new workplace, in whatever shape it takes, has the potential to bring out the best in people

by giving them what they want. As a result, higher productivity and customer satisfaction are realised. Employee expectations as a result of the epidemic suggest that businesses reassess their work processes. From the C-suite to the shop floor, employees want more meaning in their jobs.

What VUCCAD stands for?

Volatility: Volatility, in a broad sense, is frequently associated with either market volatility—quick swings and changes in company market capitalisation, frequently during swings from bull to bear markets—or volatile personalities—people prone to wild behavioural swings. Our new condition of being is one of volatility. Our politics, our social structures, and our climate have all been drastically altered by technology. We are in the process of transitioning from the old world to the new one, and volatility is one of the symptoms of that change.

Uncertainty: While it's crucial to have preparations in place to get through these crises, forward-thinking companies are also prepared to use these moments as chances to strengthen their market position and competitiveness by taking advantage of uncertainty to their advantage. The only real certainty in business settings is, well, business uncertainty.

Complexity: Complexity in business receives negative press. That is not unexpected. Understanding how a system or organisation composed of several extremely diverse interrelated pieces truly functions can be intellectually taxing. However, just because a system or organisation is challenging to comprehend does not always make it a poor one. Complexity has important advantages over its more obvious drawbacks, particularly in dynamic and unpredictable contexts. A willingness to adopt unconventional solutions, a deeper understanding of the risk factors most likely to jeopardise your operations , and the development of value-focused, proactive initiatives are all necessary to harness the power of business unpredictability. Even while it could seem like an uphill battle, putting in the time and effort can pay off handsomely both during crises and the recoveries that follow them.

Conflict: Due to problems including increased stakeholder disagreement, inadequately stated requirements, and unnecessary rework, projects without a well-defined business need tend to take longer. To save you time and effort, here are some reasons why determining the business requirement is an essential first step in any organisational transformation.

Organisational leaders' opposition to formal dispute resolution procedures frequently makes managing business conflicts more difficult. However, those that adopt the dispute system design principles are likely to discover that they can rapidly and affordably resolve internal issues. Workplace disagreements are all too prevalent in the commercial world. Think about the following examples of real-life conflicts.

- The lack of an integrated framework for handling business conflicts results in low morale and high turnover in many organisations. Rapid action in times of conflict can significantly cut down on the expense and duration of dispute settlement.

In the corporate environment, conflict may take many different shapes, some involving individuals and others involving procedures. Waiting until there is a disagreement at your company could make it impossible for you to resolve it before it hurts your business. It will be easier to spot possible issues before they happen and take preventative measures if you are aware of certain typical disputes that occur in professional settings.

Ambiguity: Ambiguity in the workplace is a complicated issue. Occasionally, ambiguity can be advantageous, but more often than not, the absence of direction and clarity stifles activity and prevents successful outcomes. Taking up uncertainty head-on boosts morale and clarifies the overall course of action. Change will always occur. Without it, everyone would become immobile. We need to adopt a development mentality, be open to ambiguity, and be prepared to welcome change if we want to advance both professionally and personally. Uncertain or unknown outcomes make ambiguous situations uncomfortable. However, your capacity to handle ambiguity will determine whether you succeed or fail. An individual who has the ability to deal with ambiguity can handle risk and uncertainty, adjust their approach with ease, adapt successfully to change, and shift gears. We label those who excel at handling ambiguity as adaptable or flexible.

Dynamism: We can better feel and react to dynamics at play across an organisation that functions as a living organism if we develop into more natural and conscious leaders. The rates at which new enterprises join the market, expand, and depart the market are used to gauge business dynamism, a crucial component of the expansion of the economy. The creation and growth of new businesses, as well as, on the other hand, their decline and market exit, are essential components of business dynamism and economic growth. Stronger dynamism is associated with higher rates of productivity growth as unproductive firms leave and more productive firms enter or grow. Thus, corporate dynamism plays a crucial role in the market structure and economic productivity, as well as serves as a catalyst for market changes.

Businesses that have specific agreements and action plans and work autonomously to attain their goals. The action instructions were co-created and disseminated by one or more people, who were accidentally amplified as a consequence of the good outcome, which, depending on the circumstances, expanded their reach. Some organisations have already done so and gone even farther (Amazon, Google, Netflix, Airbnb, WeWork, Facebook, LinkedIn, Kanbanzone, Zoom), while others are in the process. The outcomes, as well as the effort, arise from the iterative, incremental, and emergent execution.

As you've seen, organisations are always confronted with technological and adaptive obstacles. Adaptive challenges provide a more unclear problem to be solved, whereas technical challenges have a well defined problem that can be solved by professionals. Adaptive leadership as a framework can be a beneficial method to handle such issues. Furthermore, despite the hurdles that come with this strategy, building this skill allows businesses to prosper in the long run.

> *"The adaptable organisation is a fundamental shift in operating and management philosophy that allows large-scale global businesses to think like startups and drive current people practices that enable enterprise agility through empowered networks of teams."*

When an organisation adaptive in nature, it builds on its previous capabilities while generating completely new functionality. You pay homage to the past while also determining what you can let go of for the sake of adaptability. For those who are losing, the losses are severe.

The environment in the past, in more stable times, companies gained a competitive edge by making gradual efforts to become more standardised, efficient, and better at doing what they'd been doing for a long time. Organisational survival in uncertain times necessitates the knowledge that companies are part of a larger external ecosystem, bound together by a distinct, customer-centric purpose that is continually developing to remain relevant.

> "*A common purpose is the glue that holds an ecosystem together, despite ongoing iteration and adaptation. It considers the organisation's success from the perspectives of consumers, stakeholders, and society. As a result, people who are engaged in meaningful work are more likely to achieve the company's goals.*"

In these incredibly trying times, investing in and harmonising your continuous improvement efforts today might prove to be a critical move in helping you achieve a competitive edge and maximise your company's performance for tomorrow. You can learn the following from people who are adopting an ecosystem mindset:

- Businesses and organisations will eventually have to conduct their operations on a different playing field, with different rules and, in many cases, fewer teams.

- Employee safety must come first, with social isolation measures and remote working possibilities the most urgent problems to address and overcome.
- Using customer-focused missions, a bold corporate purpose cascades across the business.
- Teams work efficiently on their individual tasks without interfering with one another, but they are held together by a long-term organisational commitment.

Basic concepts for self-organisation include decentralisation of decision-making; flattening of traditional hierarchies; role changes; and the formation of agile teams, all of which imply rapid and expedient decision-making. These fundamental principles are put into practice to enable a manner of doing and concreting things; they also stem from values, which shape a style of thinking and provide higher work plan sustainability.

> *"Embracing change, having a flexible attitude, actionable thinking, learning from prior experiences, and having agile values and principles may all help us boost your chances of surviving a crisis."*

Organisations learn because they are complex, adaptive systems made up of individuals. This type of learning must be the foundation of any business. While the organisation's vision is the ultimate aim that drives it, the vision, as well as the organisation's capacity and mission, should constantly and continually be informed by learning.

- Organisational learning is the source of new capabilities and the driving force behind adaptable organisations.

Because organisational learning happens all the time, adaptive leaders must create a culture in which organisational members are acutely aware of this fundamental, continuing function.

A self-organising system forms an ordered structure based on certain suitable principles as it advances. The better a company's capacity to identify, produce, and operate new talents to efficiently adapt to its environment, the stronger its self-organisation is.

- Flexible governance frameworks are required to support an adaptable organisation. When bureaucracy is reduced, choices are clear, and individuals are empowered, governance allows for adaptive work. It is recommended to use a test-and-learn strategy to implementation. Rather of a loud explosion, the path to becoming an adaptable organisation is a succession of tiny, gradual improvements.
- In order to achieve the goal, there must be a unified emphasis on how to expand capabilities and optimise systems to enable your business to perform its job faster, cheaper, and better.
- Given how long most organisations take to make a choice and then act on it, this was an urgent need for more agility on short notice. Employee requirements, consumer expectations, and economic instability are all areas where agility is emphasised – and will continue to be.

A leadership team may select where to focus their attention, plan, and establish a stronger organisational resilience state in the future through a comprehensive evaluation. Teams execute in an iterative and empowered manner. Teams must embrace an agile, " fail fast " mindset that allows them to adapt quickly to changing client expectations through regular touchpoints, iteration reviews, and cross-team planning. Only when decision-making powers are transparent and teams are allowed freedom and autonomy is this achievable.

- Agile transformations require enthusiastic believers to help them succeed. The supporters should be well-informed and experienced practitioners who can attest to the benefits. They will aid in the development of grassroots support for the change.
- Organisational capability development refers to the ability to create, perform, or deploy resources toward a certain purpose.
- Organisations, like people, have numerous sorts of capacity. What you see is what you see with your eyes. What you do is your mission. And capacity is a level of preparedness that enables you to carry out your objective. It's a system within a system.
- Adaptable organisations must manage customer adaptation and scalable efficiency at the same time. They acknowledge the importance of both and strike a good balance by combining functional and cross-functional, centralised and decentralised teams.
- Adaptable organisations place a higher focus on the team and use team composition and new ways of working to unleash individual potential. In an adaptable organisation, good team growth looks like this: the realisation that team composition is inextricably tied to individual performance.

- Individuals can only fully prosper when their different viewpoints, distinct skillsets, and wide experience are brought together. A distinct focus that brings the team together around the organisation's mission.

Adaptive workplaces, a more fluid model that gives workers more freedom to work from wherever they are most productive, allowing them to do their best job and produce better results for employers, will likely be the way of the future.

- Organisations that prioritise employee engagement perceive increased productivity as well as other advantages such as decreased turnover and more innovation.
- Organisations with low engagement, on the other hand, have poorer productivity, more turnover, and higher degrees of burnout.
- Adaptive workspaces provide the best of both worlds in terms of increasing productivity. While government agencies are still adjusting to the fast virtualisation of work, new research shows that firms that use adaptable workplaces reap considerable organisational and labor benefits.

"The existence of pressure and tremendous obstacles is a constant for business systems in today's times, as is the standard in business."

Finally, organisational learning through feedback expands capability. Aside from that, capability must be quantifiable. This means that you must finally develop some metric for determining how effective your capacity is in terms of mission enablement. Because capability is a natural function of an organisation, the purpose of leadership is to steer it toward an enabling mission, which leads to vision.

As a result of technology's immediacy and face-to-face engagement with other latitudes, you may live internationally, but you also increase your vulnerability to hazards that were formerly global but now produce turbulence in your own environs.

How will you define a business crisis?

A worldwide crisis can increase the uncertainty and volatility in business transactions as well as in a country's economic, social, and political situation. It has direct or indirect repercussions on businesses, depending on the reason. Any unintentional, natural, or intentional event that has the potential to have a significant impact on business, people, the environment, or the local and global community as a natural or human-instigated fact that disrupts the normal operation of business systems is referred to as a crisis.

To make a breakthrough from the way you thought and acted, you should probably change your way of thinking, unlearning, and relearning; the change is not implemented only with thought, with desire; it is necessary to take action; if this action leads us to manage your company in a completely different, self-organised manner, you are preparing yourselves for almost everything.

> "*Remember that the Japanese word for crisis is opportunity for progress.Negative changes in returns, decreasing job morale, and declining incomes are all signs of a crisis.*"

The stable organisational structures may encourage order, unambiguous decision-making, and functional silos to ensure optimal efficiency when change is predictable. Traditional organisational frameworks, on the other hand, cannot keep up in an era of exponential change. What you're starting to see in terms of adaptable organisation structure and design: Both official and informal institutions must be aligned with customer-focused goals. Traditional techniques frequently compel organisations to work in a strictly functional or matrix context without considering the impact on human networks.

How will you define an effective organisational leadership?

Effective organisational leadership necessitates leaders and team members quickly focusing on executing the organisation's purpose in order to realise its vision with maximum efficiency and success. This starts with a clear, quantifiable, and attainable vision. The most succinct definition of vision is a desired future objective or condition, but a good vision must also possess a variety of additional characteristics. But first, let us explain why a vision should be a future aim or condition. Every organisation tends to progress toward a state. What differs is whether the movement is concerted, directed, and coordinated, and whether it represents a desired future condition.

The present economic crisis has also stretched the boundaries of how corporations perceive employee satisfaction. Employing such measures can be an effective way to improve employees' physical health and emotional well-being. While some firms recognised the pandemic's humanitarian catastrophe and emphasised employees' well-being as people over employees' well-being as workers, others have forced employees to work in high-risk environments with no assistance, considering them as workers first and people second.

What are the distinctive features of an adaptable organisation that thrives?

Adaptable organisations are able to identify changes in the external environment rapidly and adapt accordingly. Adaptive work frequently entails challenging an organisation's underlying assumptions, challenging the status quo, and implementing changes that may appear harsh but are required. Leaders must set their own interests aside in any tough scenario and devote their resources and efforts to the greater good. Organisations that solve these issues get a better employee experience, higher loyalty, and more access to talent pools. The new workplace, in whatever shape it takes, has the potential to bring out the best in people by giving them what they want. The adaptable organisation is a fundamental shift in operating and management philosophy that allows large-scale global businesses to think like startups.

> *"Adaptable leaders must create a culture in which organisational members are acutely aware of this fundamental, continuing function. In an adaptable organisation, good team growth looks like this: the realisation that team composition is inextricably tied to individual performance."*

Many organisations today are working to adapt to the future. I occasionally get hired to help organisations on this quest. The definition of a "future-fit organisation" is far less clear, though. An example must be given to the concept of "future-fit." It is especially pertinent at times like now, when everyone in the world is switching from one paradigm to another, in this case, from what has occasionally triggered a movement from the third to the fourth Industrial Revolution. With conveyer belts and gravity wells, Henry Ford introduced the assembly line to complex manufacturing for the first time in 1913.

As a result, assembly time decreased from 12.5 hours to 93 minutes, and the same factory that previously produced 100 cars per day could now produce 1000 in the same amount of time. Despite how significant this change was, it was nothing in comparison to what the second industrial revolution did to the world of employment.

For decades, the key to success for profit-making organisations has been to "own the supply," or to produce and distribute a sizable majority of the products or services sold in a certain market. This has been the case with a variety of products, including razor blades, baked beans, insurance, and legal counsel. This is a way to succeed in a world where entry obstacles are high . But now, that tried-and-true tactic is ineffective.

> "*The Global Lamp Index's extensive study over many years demonstrates that businesses using this living-systems strategy routinely outperform their mechanical competitors. As a result of these strategies, organisations are better able to compete and adapt in increasingly unstable business environments by attracting and keeping top employees and innovation.*"

In these increasingly unstable times, our companies' ability to thrive or even survive is really being hindered by the logic of yesterday. Therefore, even if we take a while to "get it" in terms of the mindset change that is now necessary, we discover that we are eventually obliged to do so as our monolithic machine-mentality breaks down under the pressure of constant change. Only those businesses that can adapt to this constant change will be successful in the years to come.

We must concentrate on fostering purpose, engagement, and innovation in the workplace if we are to satisfy the demands of the broader cultural transition. This encourages creativity, cooperation, and purposefulness in the core of routine meetings and decision-making, allowing people to tap into more of their inborn creative spark. Our creative potential is unlocked by these freeing methods, which also enable us to live with more purpose and awareness of the contribution we are making.

According to Mercer's 2019 Global Talent Trends report, 73% of CEOs — up from 26% in 2018 — foresee major upheaval in the coming next 5 years, and almost all of them are already taking steps to get ready.

> *"Consider a company that produces the enabling environment for life. Imagine freeing ourselves from mental enslavement for a minute. Let's let go of yesterday's attitude and free our brains. Imagine a company that improves the humanity of each of its stakeholders and contributes to the larger societal fabric in which it functions."*

Far too many companies in today's world are stuck in hierarchical, KPI-obsessed, compartmentalised, control-based, defensive, reactive, and fire-fighting mindsets that stifle the capacity to adapt and change in the face of turbulence. Increasing volatility, complexity, and unpredictability are the new norms; as a result, our businesses must be adaptable to constant change. When there is unrest, the risk is not in the unrest itself but in responding to the unrest with outdated reasoning.

How do we begin this changeover?

All of this is done in an effort to foster a workplace where employees feel free to bring their entire selves to work. Failures are turned into lessons through an adult-to-adult culture of agility and empowered entrepreneurialism, which lowers bureaucracy and anxiety.

We need to look to nature for our new leadership principles if we want to break free from these status quo structures. The old mechanical management philosophy, which is the foundation of most of today's mainstream corporate world, is fundamentally altered by leading by nature. Instead, a living systems perspective sees our organisations as living systems full of intricate processes, including human interactions, drawing inspiration from the way biology functions. We can better feel and react to dynamics at play across an organisation that functions as a living organism if we develop into more natural and conscious leaders.

How to build a resilient organisation in a VUCCAD business world?

COVID-19 has given businesses a new reality. It has prompted a significant paradigm shift, forcing companies to prepare for the future and embrace a people-first approach to the current problem. The escalating COVID-19 socioeconomic catastrophe is compelling business executives throughout the world to react quickly to the epidemic and its repercussions on their companies.

The coronavirus illness of 2019-20 has caught the globe off guard and has had a significant impact on many people's lives, especially those in the business sector and its stakeholders. Thousands of businesses have developed crisis management strategies, with many of them moving to a completely virtual workplace. Businesses have faced several obstacles as a result of the COVID-19 situation. Many businesses have already suffered financial losses, and the World Economic Forum estimates that the global economy will be affected by $1 trillion. Employers are becoming more nimble in order to tackle these challenges. Companies made significant efforts to protect employees as the COVID-19 outbreak turned into a pandemic on short notice.

While the benefits of being an adaptable organisation are obvious, conventional businesses will encounter difficulties in making the move. Moving from hierarchical to servant leadership, as well as devolving governance and decision-making to teams at the customer-facing level, poses difficulties for traditional leadership paradigms. It will be difficult for an organization to maintain a flexible mentality and culture digitally if the modular digital infrastructure can not match rising demand.

> *"Creating an agile work culture that values and supports cross-team cooperation, ownership of outcomes, and information flow necessitates various behaviors, attitudes, and abilities, which can be difficult for bigger, more complicated organisations."*

To be effective, any enterprise-wide transformation would require constant executive support and direction. A big bang approach to change, on the other hand, may be difficult in a risk-averse company climate that requires validation of success within each management cycle. Another option is to use adaptive principles to improve a specific customer-facing function. Within this business sector, new cross-functional and network-based teams aligned to particular client goals might be formed and established utilising agile approaches. Simultaneously, via training and mentorship, assist the organisation in adopting servant leadership abilities, structures, and practices. The purposeful application of leadership, governance, and decision-making with new agile teams, with proper feedback loops and escalation channels, is required.

To manage the crisis with resilience and ensure long-term business survival, successfully managing social distancing and making remote working possible has become critical. Concerns about employee engagement and productivity have obviously moved to the forefront.

> *"According to a recent LinkedIn survey, 95% of talent management professionals in India believe that employee experience is one of the most important factors influencing the future of employees and the organization as a whole."*

People analytics is a difficulty for 55% of HR directors, according to the same survey. In order to audit and analyze organisational and employee productivity, HR analytics (to make data-driven choices) has become even more vital in this new world. Gone are the days when HR's duty was confined to filling vacancies as and when they arose. The role of human resources in today's business environment is more important than ever.

The moment has arrived for a more comprehensive view of flexibility. Embracing the where, when, and how of flexibility will give you a competitive edge in recruiting fresh talent. The financial argument is clear: provide genuine freedom to keep and develop your workforce—or watch your employees go. Organisations must also find methods to reset expectations of 24/7 availability and avoid enforcing inflexible hours on employees in order to retain staff.

Organisations must have faith that the task will be completed and that workers will have enough time and energy to attend to their personal obligations and well-being. Email blackout periods were established by one big automotive business, with employees' capacity to send and receive work emails being disabled on weekends and corporate holidays.

According to the survey, employers in India are substantially more amenable to recruiting remote workers than in other Asia-Pacific nations. HR should take on a larger role. Employees in India faced lengthy shifts when working remotely, and attrition climbed 1.5 times by 2020.

According to the research, HR will now play a major role in helping enterprises simplify their operations, create their strategy, and hire more effectively, even beyond COVID-19, as hints of a second wave intensify India's remote working demands. As remote work grows more common, HR experts are increasingly advising employers to prioritize employee engagement. It's past time for businesses to rethink their approach to flexibility.

Whether it's work-life balance, physical and mental wellness, or family care, today's employees need flexibility suited to their unique requirements. As they collaborate with HR to build unique, innovative solutions for their direct reports, managers will play a crucial role in personalising flexibility for their direct reports.

Many organisations had developed their value propositions and educated their sales employees on how to sell before the COVID-19 epidemic. Many salespeople master the ability to persuade consumers that they need to buy now rather than later to remedy an issue. As a result of the COVID-19 pandemic, customers have gained the ability to resist the sales rep. The simple conclusion is that this worldwide epidemic affected all businesses and organisations, whether large or small, in some manner. The degree of influence will differ depending on the industry you work in and the exact product or service you provide. The great majority, on the other hand, will be constrained in their capacity to sell their products or services and will be under growing pressure to cut costs.

The post-COVID 19 period is characterised by turmoil and volatility in the commercial world. You have seen over the last 10 years, in the pre-COVID-19 period, that a learning organization is a major differentiator from its competitors and creates a more lively, customer-responsive culture. However, in the post-COVID- age, more is required. It has already been noticed that having a learning organisation is not enough to obtain a competitive advantage; employees must also demonstrate adaptive performance.

- Organisations are continually looking for individuals who can learn and adapt to the changing needs of the business world. As a result of technological advancements and organisational reorganisation, employees must learn new skills and improve their flexibility.
- Organisations must perform well in these area of adaptive performance for organisations to obtain

competitive advantages in the post-COVID-19 future.

- Be thoughtful in your approach and consider the long-term consequences of employee experience. If remote and on-site personnel have been treated differently, address the disparities. Engage task employees in a team culture and foster an inclusive environment.
- Organisations were already confronting greater employee expectations for openness prior to COVID-19. Employees and potential applicants will evaluate companies based on how they handled employees throughout the epidemic. Balance today's efforts to address acute pandemic concerns with the long-term impact on the employment brand.
- Assist CEOs and executive leaders in making judgments on executive pay cutbacks, for example, and ensure that the financial consequences are borne by executives rather than the entire workforce.
- Progressive organisations communicate freely and regularly to demonstrate how they support their staff despite cost-cutting efforts. Look for ways to form talent-sharing relationships with other organisations to help employees who have been displaced by COVID-19 find new employment.

> "*According to a 2019 Gartner organization design study, 55% of organizational redesigns focused on simplifying roles, supply chains, and procedures in order to improve efficiency. While this method captured efficiency, it also introduced vulnerabilities since systems are unable to adapt to interruptions.*"

The existing order has been upended by the COVID-19 epidemic, environmental concerns, and societal unrest. Organisations in all industries are being forced to change at a faster rate than ever before. Even major incumbent organisations have had to adjust to the world's largest agile working experiment during the last year, showing that old dogs can learn new tricks.

- Organisations must now be able to adjust their operations and consumer offers with breakneck speed, yet outdated systems, processes, and approaches frequently stymie them. How can they better prepare themselves to respond better and faster to become more flexible and prosper in the face of perpetual change?
- Organisations with shorter, more detailed planning horizons can repeatedly reprioritise efforts based on current needs. Leaders must be willing to adjust goals and designs when company objectives shift and feedback from early iterations emerges.
- Agile product ownership and backlog management strategies might aid in this situation, especially when making potentially emotional decisions objectively.

While the COVID-19 epidemic emphasises the importance of agility and speed in the workplace, it's critical to remember that it's not about completing everything at breakneck speed. Looking for inventive methods to enhance company resilience, future-proof income sources, improve processes, and ensure staff are well-managed and supported is what organisational agility is all about.

The encouraging reality is that people who have been dealing with fear and uncertainty for more than a year demonstrate an unbreakable spirit. Adaptive organisations' teams didn't rely on adrenaline; instead, they pushed themselves forward, appreciative of the positions they had and what they could do online if they couldn't meet their coworkers in person.

How will you find the roadblocks and challenges?

I find it intriguing that both the McKinsey and Workday studies found that organizations with integrated agile skills, such as data accessibility and cross-functional cooperation, were more likely than others to adapt quickly to the epidemic.

> "*The most successful people are those who accept and adapt to constant change. This adaptability requires a degree of flexibility and humility most people can't manage.*"

Leaders can not know whether or not their companies are actually resilient unless they are put to the test. In their 2021 Resilience Report, Deloitte highlighted five characteristics of resilient businesses, which business executives may mimic to create better resilience in their own organisations following a turbulent 2020.

What five resilience attributes may companies use to succeed in the face of adversity?

Most resilient organisations prioritise all of these characteristics, not just one or two. This is partly due to the fact that these traits frequently overlap and complement one another. To nurture and sustain them, you'll need desire, effort, investment, and action. Most significantly, the evidence indicates that speed is key. During the

COVID-19 crisis, organisations that made early investments in resilient strategies—or, even better, had previously made strategic, employees, and technological investments in resilience-enhancing capabilities—outperformed their competitors. This study demonstrates a key lesson learned from the pandemic: resilience is as much about planning ahead as it is about responding to and recovering from a disaster.

By deliberately nurturing these qualities, your company will be better positioned to overcome upheavals and bring in a new normal. Deloitte Global's fourth annual preparation study examines the topic of organisational resilience in the face of a turbulent 2020. You must be eager to hear how businesses are dealing with the unforeseen obstacles you experienced in the previous year, as well as your thoughts on what made your businesses more or less resilient to upheaval.

A secure environment for collaboration and linked working. This is accomplished through flexible communication, human connection, and alignment with the larger organisation's objective. True collaboration can help organisations achieve more agility by unlocking latent productivity and inclusiveness.

The typical "office day" has evolved. After nearly a year of the world's tremendous overnight transition to a virtual work environment, the public sector's perspective on remote and virtual work has fundamentally shifted. People may do their work swiftly, effectively, and pleasantly while working remotely, thanks to this forced move toward a dispersed and highly virtualised work environment. It has demolished the myth that employees can't be as productive while they're working remotely.

Although research into the influence of COVID-19 on organisational structure, job design, and employee well-being has increased, few studies have looked into the importance of leadership and what it takes to be a successful leader under such circumstances. Using the COVID-19 crisis as a case study, this study combines social cognition theory and conservation of resources theory to argue for the role of adaptable personalities in the creation of competent leaders during times of crisis. You contend that managers with an adaptable personality have higher levels of self-efficacy for leading during a crisis, resulting in higher motivation to lead during the COVID-19 crisis.

Furthermore, it is suggested that managers with increased motivation to lead during the COVID-19 crisis have improved adaptive performance, implying a serial mediation model in which crisis leader self-efficacy and motivation to lead during the COVID-19 crisis act as explanatory mechanisms of the relationship between the adaptive personality and the manager's performance. COVID-19 has had a significant impact on the globe in a variety of fields and businesses. Changes in the implementation of a country's education system are one of COVID-19's significant impacts.

Making headway on difficult problems COVID-19, societal difficulties, and conflicts have all necessitated making quick modifications in the previous two years. Moving forward with these complex issues puts new strains on your abilities and encourages us to develop at the cutting edge of your abilities. You'll need new tools, frameworks, and solutions to do so. explains accepting responsibility for assisting others in achieving a common goal in the face of adversity is key. The ability to remain calm in the face of adversity is crucial. That is why, in today's world, you require this style of leadership. Over the years, leadership has evolved from a technical process to a much more adaptable one, requiring figuring out how to assist people deal with uncertainty.

If the COVID-19 epidemic has taught us anything, it's that firms must be more adaptable. In order to respond to constant change, they must be able to pivot. Agility has become a catchphrase for doing things better, but it is also a commercial requirement. In difficult circumstances, I believe it is normal, even wise, to be cautious when considering new investments. When budgets are limited, the first lever that finance pulls is innovation. Nonetheless, the current scenario has not slowed many global organisations' progress toward digital transformation.

Businesses were forced to deal with unforeseen upheaval and devise solutions on the fly as a result of the epidemic. This adaptability will be critical to success in 2022. This post will explain what adaptive capability is, why it's vital, and how HR can assist leaders in embracing it. It's reasonable to assume that the epidemic threw the corporate world into disarray. Before the epidemic, the rate of change was extraordinary, but the pandemic drove it beyond normalcy. Not only did leaders have to foresee and implement their teams' success, but they also had to be adaptable in order to deal with the wide range of challenges that arose.

Resilient organisations are better equipped to adapt to change and correct course more swiftly. Design roles and structures around objectives to boost agility and flexibility, and define how processes might flex to create a more responsive company. It provides workers with a variety of positions that are adaptable and flexible so that they may gain cross-functional knowledge and training. Following the global financial crisis, global M&A activity increased, and many organisations were nationalised to avoid disaster.

To minimise and manage risk in times of change, companies will focus on growing their geographic diversification and investing in secondary markets. As operating models change, the complexity of scale and organisational management will increase, posing problems for leaders. Allow business units to tailor performance management since what works for one section of the company may not work for another.

Providing reskilling and career development support—for example, by establishing resources and building up platforms to enable insight into internal jobs—when organisational complexity affects career pathing.

The present economic crisis has also stretched the boundaries of how corporations perceive employee satisfaction. Employing such methods can be an effective strategy to improve employees' physical health and emotional well-being. Focus less on jobs — which group unrelated talents — and more on the skills needed to drive the organisation's competitive advantage and the processes that fuel that advantage to develop the workforce you'll need post-pandemic. Instead of preparing for a certain future post, encourage individuals to build crucial abilities that might offer various options for their professional advancement. Employees in crucial jobs who lack critical abilities should receive more career development help.

How to thinking ahead to invest in the future to implement long lasting organisational solutions?

Organisations must improve flexibility and adapt to the changing needs of the business world as a result of technological advancements and organisational reorganisation. Leaders must be willing to adjust goals and designs when company objectives shift. Agile product ownership and backlog management strategies might aid in this situation. While the COVID epidemic emphasises the importance of agility and speed in the workplace, it's critical to remember that it's not about completing everything at breakneck speed. Leaders who could adjust to unpredictability were differentiated from those who couldn't.

Adaptive capacity refers to a person's ability to cope with change and challenges to the status quo. It also includes how a person responds to situational circumstances with suitable actions rather than default inclinations and behaviors. When company executives recognise that the circumstances are in charge, they may choose actions that boost their adaptability. As a result, leadership becomes more adaptable. Because the future is fundamentally unpredictable, adaptable leadership is essential for long-term success.

Conventional organisation, the person in charge of making operational choices, particularly major ones, is the person at the top. The leader of flexible organisations works on creating the suitable atmosphere. The coronavirus illness of 2019 has caught the globe off guard and has had a significant impact on many people's lives, especially those in the business sector and its stakeholders.

Many businesses have been pushed to their limits, and in some cases, to the brink of bankruptcy, in the previous years. Their systems have disintegrated due to intense strain on operations, supply chains, and demand, and any notion of collaboration among their ranks has been tossed to the wind. Working in crisis mode is, of course, neither sustainable nor desirable. Many company executives are now wondering how they can maintain momentum post-crisis and ensure their firms' future adaptability.

How can people transition from crisis mode to proactive thinking?

The secret is to maintain a constant state of flexibility. Every business leader understands that in order to thrive in the long run, their organisation must adapt. The true challenge isn't effectively converting your firm on a one-time basis; it's writing the capacity to adapt and transform into the DNA of the company. It's about creating a mechanism or reaction to cope with any crisis that arises, whether it's a financial, technical, environmental, or health-related one.

How do businesses become high-performance businesses?

You all know that organisational and people skills drive financial and operational success and enable organisations to execute their plans, yet the majority of businesses have no idea how to quantify them. Future leaders with talents that are suited to future requirements are in the pipeline. Leaders in high-performance businesses have been nurtured for success by rotating through various sorts of jobs and responsibilities in various functions and areas. These organisations discover and develop prospective leaders early in their careers.

> *"According to a survey of more than 5,000 executives conducted by The Boston Consulting Group and the World Federation of People Management Associations, high-performing organisations fill 60% of top-management positions with internal candidates, while low-performing organisations fill only 13%."*

All businesses may place themselves in a better position to succeed by knowing the common strands of organisational DNA. These real-world circumstances have a role in organisational transformation, allowing flexible businesses to make progress while others struggle to establish ground rules and goals.

Adaptable businesses value themselves and the environment in which they operate. They don't strive to separate themselves from this environment; instead, they thrive in it. Survivors are highly adaptive groups. They were the ones that embraced change before it wrecked them, riding the wave while others battled against it.

Adaptable organisations are those that not only survive a change in the hope of flowing back into serenity in the current economic conditions, which are crippled by numerous lockdowns and heaving under changing restrictions every few weeks. Organisational flexibility, on the other hand, allows them to accept more of these changes and make them work by altering their working model to meet the new requirements.

The difficulty is that, despite the effort put out by business executives, most attempts to make organisations adaptive fail. My personal experience working in management and as a strategy consultant supports this. When you ask senior executives what went wrong, you'll hear the same concerns again and over: some employees inside the company neglected to accept responsibility for the transition process. People began blaming one another. Nothing was done about it when things went wrong. The metamorphosis slowed down over time.For many flexible firms, profit plans have been replaced by promises of company continuity. Many businesses put long-term aspirations on hold to meet the needs of a workforce concerned about their future, stakeholders facing unpredictable demands, and operational obstacles.

The challenge of employees planning is mitigated to some extent in industries where remote employment is available. However, it will necessitate more unlearning and upskilling. While some businesses balked at the new expectations owing to a lack of digital preparedness, purpose-driven businesses maintained spirits high and order volumes high by delivering online.

To make teleworking feasible, business agility was followed to the letter and in spirit; a variety of virtual collaboration technologies were extensively utilised; and figures were tracked with the same earnestness as before the epidemic. Several of the flexible working concepts and policy modifications implemented during the pivotal period of uncertainty and emergency firefighting are still in place. Why? simply because they provide outcomes and keep flexible businesses on track with progress.

I observe that individuals do not fight change. Instead, they fight against loss, which may take various forms, including material loss, as well as loss of competence and loyalty. When people are dealing with significant losses, they are frequently resistant to change, author explains. According to me , in adaptive settings, leaders may begin to comprehend the problem by first understanding the people. Leaders are aware of the sacrifices they are asking people to make. Even if it's only noting and naming those parts and losses, it's vital to honor them. Start visualising people's anxieties and what's at stake. Someone is afraid of losing something because you perceive the improvements you are attempting to make as generally beneficial on the surface. Keep an open mind and seek out new perspectives. It is necessary to first learn about the perspectives of those who will be affected by the change in order to create an adaptive change.

According to me, the inclusion of "uncertainty" in the concept of leadership is a plus since it means that one does not have to know all of the answers. In reality, you can't fix it yourself as a leader in an adaptive environment. All you can do is assist your group in making growth, and that is a success. Taking on a variety of challenges you survive by solving challenges that emerge in the lives of your groups, whether it's an organisation, a community, a patient, or an institution.

However, you must consider the nature of the task you are confronted with. The problem is well-known, easy to recognise, and frequently identifiable based on prior experience. The solution is well-known based on prior experience and knowledge. Obstacles are frequently restricted in terms of resources, such as time and money.

The problem is frequently unknown or difficult to define; it is linked to underlying patterns or dynamics and necessitates learning. The remedy is also unknown, necessitating learning. Those who are affected by the challenge (stakeholders), including authorities, have responsibility. The barriers are more intangible: hearts and minds, ideals, loyalty, and connections.

Adaptive difficulties are the most difficult because of the leadership techniques. According to me, adaptive change necessitates leaders successfully narrating and anchoring individuals on what will remain constant and what will need to change. There are a few more things you may do to help.

- By taking a step back, leaders may observe all of the numerous variables that surround a problem.

- Observe, pause for thought, interpret, and then intervene in the process's next stage.
- Identify what has been lost, give people time to process it, and then help them move on with their lives.
- Everyone involved in the shift is tense or disturbed in some way at any given time, according to me. Learning threshold beyond which no one learns anything or makes a difference. There is also a point at which people's tolerance for change reaches a breaking point.

The zone of productive disequilibrium, is the ideal range of suffering within which the urgency of the system pushes people to participate in adaptive management system. You make issues about individuals so often but people are merely showing various viewpoints on a challenge.

- Leaders must comprehend the opinions of others rather than taking it personally, and they must develop bridges across divides—especially with those who disagree with you or who would try to stifle or reject progress.
- You're all going through waves of uncertainty right now, and your role as leaders isn't to fix it for people; it's to help them cope with it, move through it, and discover something deeper. It is critical to implement both technical and adaptive changes. Just make sure you don't mix them up—do both.

The issue is that tighter restrictions may suffocate an organisation. In truth, management should relinquish control and allow the business the flexibility it requires to function efficiently. The concept is that management should focus on stating their goals and letting the company figure out how to get there. It might be difficult to let go of your grasp while not allowing the firm to fall apart. It must be founded on a defined set of concepts that are supported by science.

Finally, the capacity to evolve in two key ways creates a persistent competitive advantage in today's fast-paced environment. To begin, businesses must take a methodical approach to driving changes in focus, strategy, direction, structure, and culture. Second, they must have the ability to quickly respond to changing market conditions.

Change is a methodical process. Despite the high failure rate of change initiatives, a few organisations are succeeding. They make certain that the leadership team is on the same page about the organisation's goals and strategies for change, and they intentionally convey that alignment to employees layer by layer throughout the organisation.

> *"Adaptable businesses value themselves and the environment in which they operate. They don't strive to separate themselves from this environment; instead, they thrive in it."*

Adaptive change requires leaders to observe, pause for thought, interpret, and intervene in the process's next stage. Obstacles are restricted in terms of resources, such as time and money; barriers are more intangible: hearts and minds, ideals, loyalty, and connections. Adaptive difficulties are the most difficult because of the leadership techniques. Adaptive leadership may provide businesses with inventive and meaningful answers to challenging situations. My view is that who you are is the most important component in defining the type of leader you will be.

What would be the ideal approach to designing a future-fit organisation?

Effective leaders think strategically, set the tone, manage resources, foster involvement, and produce outcomes. In times of significant change, flexible businesses rely on essential individuals they can trust. An organisation concentrating on future success in major markets can arrange its operations by area rather than channel. Managers become more ambitious in using their leadership talents as their spans of influence become larger. Lean organisations have a reduced cost base, but the additional benefits of success outweigh the financial ones. Despite the high failure rate of change initiatives, a few organisations are succeeding.

Organisational design may assist businesses in improving execution and achieving strategic objectives. However, the interaction of its essential elements—structure, personal talents, responsibilities, and collaboration—must be properly organised and intimately integrated with a company's strategy and sources of competitive advantage for this to happen.

A well-designed structure should stress the most important aspects of an organisation. It is difficult to accommodate all dimensions evenly in the real world. For example, an organisation concentrating on future success in major markets can arrange its operations by area rather than channel. Even while channels did not represent the main axis in the organisation, its leaders would need to make cautious efforts to guarantee that they were receiving sufficient support. The structure of an organisation should also be dynamic, focusing on current and future objectives rather than legacy priorities.

An organisation's structure may need to be adjusted as strategy, performance, or the competitive environment change. Organisations with lean architecture may focus on meaningful work rather than coordinating. Activities that do not provide value are removed. Communication and decision-making are faster with fewer organisational levels, and senior executives have a clearer picture of day-to-day operations and consumer interactions. Managers become more ambitious in using their leadership talents as their spans of influence become larger. They don't have time to micromanage, but they may gain confidence in their leadership, coaching, and inspiring abilities. Although lean organisations have a reduced cost base, the additional benefits of success outweigh the financial ones.

How do we create businesses that are fundamentally prepared for the future?

It's time to fundamentally reevaluate how we mobilise people and use resources for beneficial purposes. The manager's position has been a key component of the conventional corporate model, along with hierarchy and an organised approach. The main duties of a manager were described in the frameworks as organising, controlling, and directing. Anyone who was not a manager was, by definition, organised, managed, and directed by them. This point of view implied that managers needed to inspire their employees because they might not be as productive as they wanted otherwise. All of this minimises the significance of intrinsic drive, which refers to the notion that someone may be extraordinarily productive just because they enjoy their work.

Managers in organisations that are prepared for the future place a greater emphasis on assisting employees in achieving autonomy, mastery, stretch, connection to purpose, and connection to others than they do on organising, managing, and directing them.

You are enthusiastic about empowering individuals and organisations to thrive in the face of continual and disruptive change, and you accomplish this via programs that address organisational change, resilience, agility, leadership, transformation, and adaptation. Strong organisations are what make the difference for successful businesses.

How to encourage people's freedom to participate in a collective vetting process?

The way things are done in a organisation reflects the habits and attitudes of its employees. It is an organisation's "secret sauce," bringing a plan to life or killing it. Culture is not set in stone. Cultivating a distinct culture is both achievable and important. Employee engagement, on the other hand, is defined as employees' desire to go above and beyond for a company, not only out of responsibility or for monetary gain, but because work is important to them personally and professionally.

"An organisation's ability to learn, and translate that learning into action rapidly, is the ultimate competitive advantage."

Leadership, design, people, and change management are not the same as culture and engagement; culture and engagement are results of the other traits. In the same way that people strengthen their hearts by exercising other bodily muscles, organisations enhance culture and engagement indirectly by working on other traits.

Performance management systems, for example, which are part of the people dimension, may have a significant influence on culture. Culture helps achieve strategic goals faster. A good organisational culture does not happen by chance. To accomplish strategic goals, high-performance businesses establish, maintain, and monitor a culture.

A risk-averse, process-oriented culture with clear lines of authority may be perfectly logical for an airline, but it's a formula for poor performance in an Internet corporation. At each particular time, a organisation's culture either works or doesn't work for a certain company.

> *"Culture should evolve in tandem with strategic aims."*

COVID-19 has taught business executives anything, it is the difficulty of leading an organisation that is not adaptable and flexible in turbulent times. Businesses were forced to deal with unforeseen upheaval and devise solutions on the fly as a result of the epidemic. This adaptability will be critical to success in 2022 and going forward.

It's reasonable to assume that the epidemic threw the corporate world into disarray. Before the epidemic, the rate of change was extraordinary, but the pandemic drove it beyond normalcy. Not only did leaders have to foresee and implement their teams' success, but they also had to be adaptable in order to deal with the wide range of challenges that arose.

This ushered in a new age for business, one in which the ability to adapt is crucial to existence. Businesses can no longer rely on traditional long-term strategic direction-setting to compete and expand in an unpredictable, complicated, and ambiguous world.

"Today's businesses must be able to detect emerging market changes fast and respond swiftly to take advantage of prospective opportunities or resist emerging dangers."

Adaptive businesses have the technical and organisational agility to do so, and workplace settings that support resilience, deeper levels of engagement, motivation, cooperation, and autonomy result in improved performance and employee retention.

- Is your company prepared to react to shifting conditions outside your control?
- What can you do as a leader to help your company become more adaptable?

Every time your organisation overcomes an adaptable problem, it expands its adaptive capacity and becomes more prepared and equipped to face the next adaptive challenge. You may also improve your organisation's adaptability by fostering a flexible culture.

Instilling learning culture is another technique to make an organisation more adaptive. The rapidity of change, as well as the influence of fast globalisation, is a problem for adaptive companies. They attempt to stay one step ahead of their industry's competitors. It is critical to behave effectively and efficiently in addition to working quickly and harder.

The only way to behave wisely is to reflect on both accomplishments and mistakes and share lessons learned with all employees. This gives front-line staff the perspective of top executives, which can help them make rapid judgments when they're required the most.

"In order to achieve company goals, being flexible is preferable to being process-focused."

It is critical to promote responsibility in order to achieve adaptation. It's always simpler to blame success on hard work and blame failure on bad luck, but flexible businesses prioritise cultivating and developing a culture of self-accountability. The sense of responsibility guarantees that each member completes obligations with dedication. It fosters a culture of trust and assists the company in avoiding passing on techniques and blame games.

Furthermore, the system's viewpoint instills accountability since employees recognise that their actions have consequences. A good organisational culture does not happen by chance. To accomplish strategic goals, high-performance businesses establish, maintain, and monitor a culture. A risk-averse, process-oriented culture with clear lines of authority may be perfectly logical for an airline, but it's a formula for poor performance in an Internet corporation.

At each particular time, a company's culture either works or doesn't work for a certain company. Personal motivators, like recognition, and performance disciplines, such as performance management measures, are at the core of employee engagement. High-performance organisation keep an eye on their employees' pulses, assessing engagement levels on a regular basis and actively managing engagement during challenging periods like restructuring or large-scale change initiatives.

Organisations with high performance just operate differently. They recognise the importance of having all traits in their company and work together to put them in place. They also determine which of their trait is the most important for long-term competitive advantage and strive to strengthen weak areas through a systematic set of initiatives and activities.

It all begins with the Board of Directors (BOD) agreeing that this is the sort of culture they want to see developed. Following agreement, specific procedures must be performed to begin the implementation process.

Leaders and managers must collaborate. Leaders and managers must work hard to build a culture of choice, which may be aided by having a description of the current culture in place. An adaptive corporate culture enables a company to respond swiftly and effectively to internal and external change demands. A business culture that continuously promotes a healthy psychological environment will make employees more stress-resistant. Such a workforce will be able to adjust to change successfully while maintaining productivity.

Any organisation using the methods detailed in the wellbeing and performance agenda must adopt the concepts of adaptive leadership as a top priority, and no change in attitude or practice will occur until someone or several individuals take the initiative. Two elements that underpin the culture of the organisation are psychological responsibility and sharing responsibility for the organisation's future success.

They have an impact on how individuals interact with one another. Following adaptive leadership, these two agenda items should be implemented. The components of culture that substantially impact trust, commitment, motivation, kinship, focus, and social engagement, the traits that constitute psychologically healthy organisations that function at their peak, are added to adaptive corporate culture.

A culture is made up of several components, all of which contribute to the tone, mood, and expectations that surround the workforce and impact their attitude and approach to work.

> *"An adaptable corporate culture that affects the organisation's health and is one that is purposefully developed to generate the tone, mood, and expectations of a psychologically healthy organization, one that encourages employees to feel good."*

Culture is strong, but it may feel intangible, like a mystery cloud — that while workers, customers, and partners come and go at different times, an organisation's culture endures. The issue is, is culture something that can be consciously built? And the answer is yes, you can construct it and modify it on purpose. When it comes to culture, success is usually due to the sharing of mental models, particularly the most significant mental models such as vision, mission capacity, and learning, among others. And if you don't, you're left with a few well-written sentences and a few maps. Culture occurs when individuals share the same mental models.

The CEO of the organisation creates and implements a common framework for organisational learning in order to maintain their original startup adaptability as they grow into a larger organisation in a rapidly changing environment. And, like many organisations, they began as a small team with spontaneous and intimate contact and a rapid synthesis of ideas into action.

As the organisation expanded to more than 200 people and had a complete management team, conflicting viewpoints on the company's strategic goals began to translate into disparate and unconnected approaches to operational duties.

In other words, they were experiencing growing pains. Everyone was working hard, but not all in the same direction.They desired assistance with increasing clarity around their vision and goals; getting everyone in the company on the same page; and identifying and defining organisational capabilities and learning processes.

Design, develop, and implement leadership development programs that are iteratively designed, developed, and deployed by the leaders who engaged in steps one through three above. Iterate material based on the most important aspirations and intents.

Leaders must be re-engaged in order to continue their education. Engage learners in refining learning content as the deployment continues by giving application examples, new application scenarios, and hazards. Baseline indicators of employee engagement and sentiment, such as individual experiences with diversity, equity, and inclusion, job value, leadership quality, and teamwork, are used to assess effects.

Adaptive Organisations' Leadership Roles When members of the C-suite, talent management, people leaders, and individual contributors (such as subject matter experts) who lead without direct reporting and L&D professionals work together, successful programs emerge.

- They actively participate in the development of leaders by teaching, coaching, and mentoring others.
- They achieve and sustain desired team and individual results.
- They take responsibility for your own growth and make use of the resources available to you.

- They look for chances to display, improve, and apply skills. Professionals in learning and development assist trainees in addressing the specific concerns and challenges that leaders face.
- Combine behavioral and technical skills, as well as do-it-yourself and learn-as-you-go learning.
- Transformation must begin inside the CLO, L & D, and other people management professionals if they are to effectively construct adaptable companies.

Incorporate critical thinking, diversity, and other behavioral competencies into the curriculum and learning environment. CLO and L & D professionals add value by empowering and mentoring organization leaders at all levels, regardless of title or tenure. The C-suite adds value by keeping the company's strategy and goals up-to-date and clear. In this new model, CLOs and L & D professionals add value by empowering and mentoring organisational leaders at all levels.

Consider the following developing principles to respond to opportunities and disruptions, cross-functional teams must adjust all organisational systems, including incentives and recognition, talent management, and learning and development. Start with your own internal knowledge and skills. When you've found adaptable leaders, search for leadership, technology, and management knowledge from outside sources to continue expanding your adaptive leadership schema. To help you scale, create a leadership team with a single leadership system attitude. Integrate organisational leadership competence and capacity into leaders' daily work flows.

Adaptive businesses have the technical and organisational agility to do so, and workplace settings that support resilience, deeper levels of engagement, and autonomy result in improved performance and employee retention.

Instilling learning is another technique to make an organisation more adaptive. Culture reflects the habits and attitudes of a company's employees. A good organizational culture does not happen by chance.

> *"A culture that encourages individuals to feel good and motivates them to achieve peak performance motivates them to be extremely successful."*

Adaptive leaders strike a compromise between their ideal vision of what they want to achieve and the realities of teachers' lives. This intermediate ground is exemplified by the huddle-call structure, which allowed instructors to collaborate on problems but didn't compel them to coordinate their improvement efforts. The Goldilocks zone has the advantage of being long-term and may lead to modest improvements.

We're running out of time. We need to take drastic action and address underlying problems while also paying attention to downstream repercussions if we want to assure anything like a good conclusion for our organisations, larger socio-economic systems, and general civilization. Such a change puts us to the test on fundamental, often unconscious levels. It questions significant and intricate effects that exist in our own psyches and societal consciousness.

> *"An agile organisation adjusts swiftly to an ever-changing environment."*

A future-fit organisation constantly asks itself how it can give clients a nexus (not just a product) and the most seamless manner to satisfy their demands through the use of technology. In order to be as sensitive to the context of the consumer as feasible, it also considers how to be as close to the client as possible. Contrary to popular belief, organisations that are motivated by a higher purpose outperform those that are driven by financial gain, according to several studies. The goal generates a potent combination of inner and extrinsic drive, which accounts for the impact's extraordinary magnitude. It connects to our needs for purpose, kinship, and participation.

"The interior dimensions of organisations include their mission, culture, values, meeting customs, and decision-making procedures that support their way of being. By trying to enhance these, we may develop a meaningful, entrepreneurial, self-managing, and inclusive manner of working."- Dr. Amit Das

Reshaping The Future Of Work Experience

"The reasonable man adapts himself to the world; the unreasonable one persists in trying to adapt the world to himself. Therefore all progress depends on the unreasonable man."
-George Bernard Shaw

A future-fit organisation starts by establishing its mission. This is about making purpose the DNA of the organisation, from long-term strategy to day-to-day operational decision-making, not just having a purpose statement, though this may be a valuable tool. The emphasis on the description, monitoring, and analysis of operations increased with the development of scientific management. The activity-based perspective has endured even though scientific management is basically outdated.

"A deeper sense of purpose that resonates with us on a soul level because we are clear on our part in producing genuine value for ourselves, each other, and our more-than-human planet is what helps link these scattered, networked, self-organizing, locally attuned teams."
- Dr. Amit Das

Apple may be the company that does this the best. Despite producing only 18% of the world's cellphones, they take home 86% of the industry's profits. Nobody wonders how much it costs to make an iPhone because they are willing to pay a high price for the benefits they perceive the product to offer. Only 18% of cellphones worldwide are sold by Apple. However, it earns 51% of all smartphone sales worldwide. and accounts for 86% of global smartphone earnings! The greatest way to develop, deliver, and collect value is where a future-fit organisation starts.

The activities are then coordinated to correspond. The first three shifts discuss the organisation's core values and winning strategies. The organisation's structure will be discussed during the final four shifts in order to make it a reality. Understanding this causal flow is crucial because the remaining alterations aren't just happening by accident; rather, they're being developed to help organisations flourish in a setting that differs from the one they were used to.

The hierarchy, which is often represented as a series of boxes and reporting lines, is maybe the most enduring emblem of the corporate period. It has long been believed that hierarchy, which is established through vesting authority, is a source of efficiency.

> *"Once more, I discover that organisations that were future-ready have chosen a different course. They may not have completely abandoned hierarchy, but they have flattened their organisations."*

For instance, the central organisational unit of Spotify is a small, independent team of no more than eight individuals. Each team is responsible for a certain component of the product, which it owns from conception through disposal. Squads are in charge of choosing what to construct, how to build it, and who to collaborate with in order to make the final product compatible. Another illustration is Zappos, which employs "circles" that anyone may apply to join in addition to their standard function through a "Role Marketplace." You go up in front of a group of people rather than your immediate supervisor to ask for recompense. These team-based or network-based systems and conventional hierarchies vary primarily in that they are driven by volunteering rather than authority.

In addition, it is more quick-witted and adaptive, which brings us to the next change. Another technique that has been mastered over the last century is planning, whether it is for the development of a new product or the launch of a significant project. Everything needed to be mapped out from the beginning, down to the specific details of the finished features. Then software developers realised it wasn't functional.

According to the analysis, there is a "cone of uncertainty" where initial estimates are sometimes four times too high or too low. Due to the paradigm being reversed such that time and cost would be set but features may change, this gave rise to the Agile movement. Rapid prototyping and iterative improvements were also emphasised. This was so successful that organisations began to question if the ideals and guiding principles of Agile might be used more widely. Agile techniques, or simply "agile" ways, have been discovered to provide many benefits in a range of circumstances, as studies like the one below illustrate.

"A future-fit organisation addresses the uncertainties inherent in the problem it's trying to solve rather than pretending they don't exist, whether it uses Agile in its formal definition or just accepts its key concepts."

Consider the companies that have emerged during the past five years: AirBnB, Uber, Amazon, Google, or AliBaba. These companies lack supply-side dominance. In fact, a large number of them don't even own the products or services they offer. Instead, they offer a platform that allows buyers (and sellers, in certain situations) to easily obtain the goods they want or need to buy. The shift from supply-led to demand-led has produced economic efficiency, much like how improved supply chain management helped Wal-Mart surpass other retailers via higher production decades ago.

"We struggle to see the forest for the trees because of how busy we are and how these projects seem like unrelated subjects fighting for our attention. But the more aware we are of the tectonic upheavals these surface waves represent, the more equipped we are to assist in making our companies future-proof."

Consider how the ride-share experience has almost completely outperformed the traditional taxi sector in terms of choice, transparency, and fairness. Although the commercial sector has been completely transformed by this, the public and non-profit sectors are also affected. The truth is that today's citizens are more connected and well-informed than ever before, which is problematic for government organisations. These residents frequently use Amazon or Airbnb, so it goes without saying that they anticipate it in all aspects of life, including the delivery of government services.

In the 2019 Global Talent Trends research, almost all of the organisations that were asked are actively embracing change: 99% of participating companies say they are taking steps to prepare for the future of work. Companies are preparing for this in part by developing an integrated people strategy that balances investment in the future with attention to today's demands.

What then is the corporate world's future?

It's true that there isn't a cookbook solution that works for everyone. There will be several designs for numerous, constantly shifting landscapes. We can, however, highlight a significant change that is taking place, a change from "organisation as machine" to "organisation as living system."

> *"According to business expert Peter Senge, this business transition in logic from machine to living systems is the most significant challenge facing our leaders, managers, and change agents today."*

In practise, this entails setting up the circumstances so that our teams are better equipped to adjust locally and deal with constant change without having to rely on hierarchies of bureaucracy and control. It involves our accepting liberating frameworks and methods that go beyond the flaws in much of today's decision-making and oppressive society. Without a profound soul-sense of why we are here and the value we are adding to the larger fabric of life, and that's not to argue that some of the control-based techniques we use now won't be useful in the future. By bringing our left and right brain hemispheres into balance, bringing our mind and heart into line, and attuning our ego-attention with our soul-wisdom, we may open ourselves up to more of our humanity without tossing the baby out with the bathwater.

To put it in an easier way, picture a company that provides actual value rather than a limited definition that only helps a select few at the expense of the many. a company whose main goals are to provide real value, improve people's lives, and leave the garden in better condition than when we found it. Think about it. Offering more diversified benefits is the top goal for employcc rewards, according to the Global Talent Trends report. This outcome is hardly surprising, given that businesses are increasingly realising that innovation holds the key to success.

What does this indicate, and how can businesses promote innovation?

Instead of using a general one-size-fits-all strategy, it begins with studying and developing the numerous employee personas inside a business, and then constructing a rewards programme for each. The dissemination of information about these incentive programmes via employee-relevant channels is equally crucial. Top talent will be drawn to the employers with the most alluring benefits.

Employers are actively looking for new and innovative benefits ideas, particularly in Asia, to help differentiate their employer brand. Investments in incentives should mirror a company's strategic objective in order to fully align the business. To meet both the demand for new talents and the changing demands of employees, this frequently entails shifting away from market standards and toward more distinctive offers.

- Employers need to know what their employees value most in a job and be aware of their struggles and experiences at work. To establish a work atmosphere that appeals to the future workforce, employers must begin investing in the experiences they offer to their staff.

But where do you even begin?

This entails restructuring work and relocating personnel to areas where new value will be produced. To allow HR to carry out these crucial transformation activities with better efficiency, flexibility, and speed, it also necessitates rethinking the HR lifecycle to make it more agile.

> *"This means that businesses should focus on developing the leadership, culture, competence, and skills necessary for a competitive edge in the future."*

Leading companies are focusing on the total pay experience, going beyond base salary to include career advancement, rewards, and recognition. Only 33% of the organisations I studied can pinpoint the primary factors influencing engagement, despite more than half (54%) regularly conducting engagement surveys.

Organisations that do so use both hard and soft techniques to bring about change. Individual accountability and metrics are defined, and individuals are given the tools and power they need to succeed in implementation. They keep track of their progress against key milestones, recognize when projects are running late, and take remedial action. In order to preserve trust, they also interact and engage with important stakeholders.

Companies frequently make changes to their organisation and people aspects in response to external events, hiring more people during good times, laying off employees during bad times, and then offering leadership training when morale eventually drops and the organisation experiences whiplash reactions. Others have a more laid-back style with few proactive measures. Neither of these procedures produces consistently good results.

What really actually motivates engagement?

Giving workers the chance to upskill and/or reskill increases their sense of mastery, provides them with the opportunity to learn something new, and allows them to refine existing talents.

"Opportunities for growth and learning are essential for many workers."

It's also crucial to provide workers the freedom to make more deliberate career decisions and to feel autonomous in their employment. Through internal gig platforms or mobility programmes, where employees may put their skills to use and acquire new experiences, for instance, firms can offer people new avenues to advance by curating careers. Employers may promote and support the development of the broad skills and flexible mentality necessary for the workplace of the future.

- Preparation is essential to thinking methodically about the opportunities that lie ahead and quickening the transition to the future of work as society embraces a digital future.

- In today's fast-paced environment, the goal is to increase internal productivity by forging deeper connections with the outside world.

This entails developing strong bonds with clients, partners, the academic community, and governments, and maintaining those bonds over time. Instead of focusing on how individual teams engage with today's clients, a future-fit culture should focus on how the company scales to become a responsible firm that meets short-and long-term objectives. A healthy community encourages and stimulates a forward-thinking firm to produce new advancements and ideas since it is full of variety and inclusion.

- Building creative workplaces and giving individuals the freedom to work without interference from command and control structures will improve future fitness. Community interactions should occur spontaneously using whatever form of communication, whether in person or online, seems right at the time given the limits.

Organisations that are future-ready gauge their success by the value that innovative solutions provide for their stakeholders, while also taking into account market relevance, strategy alignment, and the effects on the environment, society, and governance. Building the plane while in flight enables the company to constantly seize new chances since reflection and learning occur naturally, and a new path is determined as necessary.

- Organisations that are future-ready work to develop a strategic portfolio of noteworthy innovations that may be used to manage their business today and into the future.

To detect blind spots and investigate opportunities, one must continually generate insights through a discovery process that takes into account new trends, laws, and governance. Through contacts with the community, new ideas and working methods are developed that aid the organisation in fulfilling its objective.

In order to produce sustainable value that is conscious of social implications, it is imperative to proactively evaluate new trends and technologies. This is how change is sought. It takes discipline to be able to move quickly when necessary and then move slowly when necessary. Being future-fit requires a combination of 100-meter sprints and ultra-marathons, which must be meticulously planned and carried out over time, or delivered with remarkable agility, depending on the circumstance. Changemakers who are persistent in inventing for the future do so by planning ahead to maintain their creativity, adaptability, and resilience while completing the work that is important now.

"If businesses want to stay competitive, new workforce strategies are required given the abrupt shift in perception of the business environment of the future. It's more important than ever for businesses to rethink their people agenda in order to unlock human potential and embrace new tactics in order to be prepared for the future as the speed of change quickens and we transition into a new world of work."

- Dr. Amit Das

The future-fit attitude is one that a freeform organisation seeks to acquire in order to become anticipatory and to have a laser-like concentration on bringing about the next paradigm change. For people who embrace future-fit values in their daily activities and use the guiding principles to change the world around them, there are many potential futures.

The "future-fit" perspective enters the picture here. This may sound intimidating, but it basically means that a company is guided by social and environmental consciousness, and this mindset drives how the company operates.

Have you prepared?

According to my study, giving workers meaningful work experiences fosters their development and success. What I observe more and more is that these job situations are greatly facilitated by empowerment. The performance of their organisation will be boosted by leaders who succeed in achieving these goals.

"Building a coherent sense of identity and purpose and encouraging workers' feelings of connection inside the workplace and to the firm are vital to creating a 21ˢᵗ-century employee experience because people also want work that is driven by purpose and want to be a part of something larger."

- We have more time to spend exploring our authenticity and pursuing our curiosities. More time to create fulfilling connections; to truly experience the universe and everything in the present moment. We have more time to appreciate life's basic pleasures and spend quality time with friends, family, and random folks we encounter on the road. However, a lot of the time, our professional lives rob us of what we value the most: the time and freedom to develop into the sociable, fun, creative, loving, and meaningful beings that we are at our core.

It challenges the ingrained patterns of power relations, dominant modes of leadership, management, and operation inside our businesses, as well as the status quo governance structures. It puts into question how we interact with one another as humans in our world of the superhuman.

> *"It may seem intimidating, but there is good news: this deep and profound transformation is nothing more or less than an exposure of who we truly are."*

- Isolated programmes such as "wellness at work," "purposeful business," "mindfulness," and "corporate social responsibility" (CSR) may not address an organisation's core assumptions, culture, and ethos. Only a thorough revision of the underlying assumptions will allow our future companies to thrive in these transformative times.

> *"It is a challenging, uncertain, freeing, and incredibly exciting moment to be part of business's future."*

Whatever the initiative, whether it be the move toward more purposeful business, addressing climate change, embracing the digitised millennial generation, CSR, wellbeing at work, diversity in the workplace, the future of work, employee empowerment, stakeholder engagement, etc., there is a deeper underlying metamorphosis of epic proportions that underpins and weaves all of these initiatives together.

We still need to complete the task at hand, keep track of to-do lists, project manage and engineer solutions, and deliver on time and within budget, but we also need to give ourselves more room to be imaginative, exploratory, and adaptable. We also need to be able to have difficult conversations in an authentic manner and to listen intently to what our collective intelligence is saying. Finally, we need to be able to recognise the synchronicities of emerging pathways amid complexity.

I've had the good fortune to work with several outstanding CEOs and organisations, and I've created a straightforward set of principles and tools that assist businesses in embracing natural systems. These tools have "inner" and "outer" aspects, and addressing each of these can assist in promoting regenerative business practises that can solve the difficulties.

This promotes interactions between adults and releases regenerative potential. The "outside dimension" in this context refers to the organisation's external communications, including its goods and services, supply chains, and stakeholder interactions on a larger scale. The development of different stakeholder relationships through the goods, services, and experiences we provide is made possible by achieving an inner-outer organisation that is cohesive.

Thanks to this emancipating change in reasoning, we may now experience what it truly means to be completely human in our companies of the future.

How to establish an organisational mindset and environment for future leadership development?

The definition of leadership is someone who enjoys making decisions and is concerned about whether their judgments will result in desirable results in the face of uncertainty. Whether a leader is equipped for core, effective, or adaptive leadership depends on how comfortable and enjoyable it is for them to make difficult unilateral decisions. How many times have you heard a leader remark, *"That's policy,"* without telling you where it says so or letting you know what you can anticipate from the policy?

Adaptive leaders aren't afraid of failure. Adaptive leaders create environments that encourage experimentation, learning, and reflection on both success and failure. Adaptive leaders and their teams become more resilient as a result of their adaptability. They get stronger as a result of their blunders. Leaders who keep going and endure in the face of adversity attain success. When they stop trying, they call it "failure."

Failure is viewed as a learning opportunity by adaptive leaders, and experimentation is praised even if the desired objective is not reached. The important thing is to keep going ahead. It's critical to figure out why something failed quickly and then move on.

If they aren't making errors, the adaptive leader believes they aren't working hard enough. Successful corporations that accept failure are Netflix, Amazon, and Coca-Cola. You can't learn unless you fail, and you can't achieve until you face obstacles. Adaptive leaders allow everyone to make mistakes. It will re-energise a company.

Leadership is in short supply in both developed and emerging sectors, where aging executives are leaving and new markets are struggling to keep up with fast development. Because of today's rapid speed of change, command and control leadership has become obsolete.

Effective leaders think strategically, set the tone, manage resources, foster involvement, hold people accountable, and produce outcomes. In good times, let alone in uncertain ones, there are no simple techniques. Leadership begins at the top of the pyramid but does not end there. Three major levers are used by high-performance businesses to develop leaders at all levels. Leaders in high-performance teams generate urgency and direction. Complexity, volatility, and change are all familiar to leaders. They can mobilise the organisation in the face of uncertainty. Although imaginative leaders are required, they cannot be lone wolves or independent operators; the heroic corporate leader's days are past.

Today's leaders must collaborate with their colleagues and appreciate the collective power that comes from teamwork. They must increasingly be at ease working with outsiders such as nonprofit groups, regulators, and other bodies that are more involved in business.

> "*Avoid placing individuals in situations where they are forced to carry out a predetermined set of chores without having any input on those tasks. That is unhealthy for your business and oppressive for them.*"

Since the world is going through so many changes, those of us in business must always consider our human resources and the value of developing leadership skills in our employees if we want to ensure that our businesses are always ready to face the difficulties that these changes provide.

Now that I own a business that concentrates on workforce and leadership skills, I am asked this question more frequently than before. Let's start with what you don't do, which is confine individuals to carrying out a predetermined set of activities without allowing them to have any influence on those tasks. That is harmful to your company and oppressive to them.

How exactly do you develop leaders?

You must foster a culture in your organisation that encourages the growth and demonstration of leadership abilities. Perhaps even more crucially, you must motivate your staff to collaborate and participate rather than just obey your instructions. The good news for future leaders is that younger generations, especially members of Gen Z, are eager to learn. They desire to advance in their roles. They also want to understand how their skills and efforts fit into the bigger picture. They want to be able to clearly understand how their own time and skill investments are making a difference. In addition, retention issues decrease when you provide them with the kinds of possibilities they want.

What exactly distinguishes a good leader—or potential leader—from others?

Those that rise to leadership positions naturally within a company typically exhibit the traits listed below:

- They are aware of and work for the organisation's purpose.
- They are aware of successful organisational behaviour.
- They may draw on a network of people, which has the effect of increasing their power and expertise.
- They have an optimistic outlook.

- Instead of claiming sole ownership of their successes, they are eager to share them.

So here's the problem: in order to cultivate leaders within your company, you must foster a corporate culture that enables these leaders to emerge and gives them the chance to develop their leadership abilities.

How to start doing it is as follows?

- Ensure that everyone is aware of the company's objective.
- It's time to write a mission statement if you don't already have one.
- If no one can identify the aim or goal, it is challenging to create a unified staff that is working toward it.
- Your whole employees should be aware of and committed to the business mission. Additionally, you must ensure that the personnel are familiar with the company structure and how it operates.
- Everyone will then be able to observe how their efforts contribute to and enhance the total. to encourage teamwork and professional development. Start by encouraging thankfulness and care throughout the company.

> *"People don't care how much you know until they know how much you care, stated President Theodore Roosevelt."*

- Share your accomplishments with your team.
- Recognise when people go above and beyond what is expected of them or when a team works together to

accomplish something exceptional.

- Encourage people inside the company to express gratitude within their own teams.
- If someone's assistance is appreciated, they are more likely to offer assistance in the future.
- Keep in mind that employees who feel their efforts are valued are more likely to be engaged than those who do not.
- Promote the exchange of ideas. Everyone should feel free to express their opinions without worrying about being mocked.

In a society where ideas are exchanged, different viewpoints frequently result in better goods and processes, but hearing ideas does not obligate you to act on them. Consider training your team in active listening techniques. The buy-in you gain by enabling a team to build a solution on their own or with their input, as opposed to being handed a solution and instructed to implement it, will more than offset the little time it takes to ensure everyone has a chance to be heard. Look for leaders to emulate.

Ask your employees to name influential people both inside and outside of your company who exhibit the traits or abilities of capable leaders that they desire to develop in themselves. Opportunities to adopt those qualities should come after this. In this particular region, copying need to be actively encouraged.

- Recognise how the mindset of your current leadership team affects your staff. Energy spreads easily.
- Encourage your team leaders to be aware of the vibe they bring into a space. Your team looks to its leaders for guidance, and one aspect of the direction that will be

taken away is the enthusiasm that they offer.

"A person with a "can-do" attitude will inspire their group. Someone with a "can't do" mentality will hinder the team."

Leadership abilities can be developed, and hands-on experience is the greatest method to do it. Therefore, it is imperative that you create an atmosphere that encourages employee empowerment so that they may acquire the skills necessary to advance their careers and, in turn, advance your business.

Do you have any leadership challenges?

Hesitancy change can only be successful if everyone in the organisation is involved in its execution. Some employees may be unwilling to execute a new approach because it requires them to master a new method or alters the nature of their work. It is possible that a new strategy will be unsuccessful if it is not applied across the whole organisation. Power adaptive leadership transfers authority and influence from a few top-level executives to all employees. Some top-level workers who are accustomed to wielding a great deal of decision-making authority may find it difficult to give control to the entire group.

While maintaining a positive environment, adaptive leadership may provide businesses with inventive and meaningful answers to challenging situations. Adaptive leadership, on the other hand, can provide a number of obstacles, including: adaptive leadership necessitates the participation of all members of the organisation. This implies adaptable leaders must urge everyone engaged to change their mentality and display adaptive leadership skills.

Employees who prefer the status quo and have no desire to change the company may find this difficult. Adaptive leadership's proactive character necessitates the recognition that some of the organisation's existing business processes are unproductive. Adaptive leadership, poses a number of difficulties. Experimenting, learning new information, and making multiple modifications throughout your organisations are all part of this leadership paradigm. You will only be able to maintain the changes and prosper if you modify your mindset and adjust your policies.

Changing people's attitudes, beliefs, and perceptions, on the other hand, is frequently more difficult than flossing a cat's teeth. Making adjustments necessitates a degree of disloyalty to your past. If you wish to adopt a new marketing plan, for example, you must first accept the truth that your current marketing techniques are ineffective.

Another issue with adaptive leadership is that it creates an environment conducive to various types of opposition. This might be from your employees or other stakeholders in the organisation. Stakeholder Any individual, group, or entity with an interest in an organisation and the effects of its activities is referred to as a stakeholder in business.

Marginalising, distracting, and assaulting are the most prevalent techniques used to stymie adaptive change. If you see any of these behaviors, it's likely that your staff are resisting the new policy you're attempting to impose. The refusal of leaders to listen to other people's perspectives is perhaps the biggest obstacle posed by adaptive leadership. Adaptive leadership, as previously said, is more about cooperation than it is about power.

Treating an adaptive task as a technical challenge is one of the most common leadership blunders. Leadership requires knowing when to solve problems and when to learn. I feel, we often look for technical answers to problems. But there's also all the adjusting that has to be done. It does not tackle the problem at its root without adaptive work. Identifying the fundamental difficulties in an adaptive challenge focuses on areas where individuals may differ, and this disagreement becomes a roadblock to development. In this instance, leaders must evaluate the following factors: competing values or priorities which are legacy issues that must be addressed. Issues or procedures that remain ambiguous or perplexing over time.

Recognising our genuine inner and outer natures is necessary for leaders. The personality we have inside is what enables us to lead with sincerity, coherence, and purpose. These principles, which I refer to as "the outer dimension" and which must be employed in conjunction with the ability to stay open and responsive to the ever-changing nature of life, are necessary for effective leadership. As a result, real environments are created where responsiveness, trust, and developmental learning flourish. Through our interactions with others, this "inner-outer" leadership strategy enables us to foster regenerative corporate settings as well as regenerative potential in ourselves.

One of adaptive leadership's strengths is also one of its limitations. For the most part, an adaptable leader must place less value on structure in order to efficiently execute change. Some employees, on the other hand, thrive in regimented workplaces, and adaptive leadership would be a poor match for them. An adaptable leader will attempt to provide some structure for those employees that require it. Nonetheless, in this unstructured work environment, there are still possibilities for individuals to be less productive.

It's in the nature of rules to be broken. An ethical leader may squirm after seeing how an adaptable leader operates. Ethical leaders support an organisation's policies because they correspond with their own personal beliefs. An adaptable leader, on the other hand, may bend (or even break) the laws within the bounds of the law in order for the business to undertake the most effective change plan feasible.

> *"Accepting responsibility for assisting others in achieving a common goal in the face of adversity is key. The ability to remain calm in the face of adversity is crucial. That is why, in today's world, you require this style of leadership. Over the years, leadership has evolved from a technical process to a much more adaptable one, requiring figuring out how to assist people deal with uncertainty."*

Although research into the influence of COVID-19 on organisational structure, job design, and employee well-being has increased, few studies have looked into the importance of leadership and what it takes to be a successful leader under such circumstances. Using the COVID-19 crisis as a case study, this study combines social cognition theory and conservation of resources theory to argue for the role of adaptable personalities in the creation of competent leaders during times of crisis. You contend that managers with an adaptable personality have higher levels of self-efficacy for leading during a crisis, resulting in higher motivation to lead during the COVID-19 crisis.

Furthermore, it is suggested that managers with increased motivation to lead during the COVID-19 crisis have improved adaptive performance, implying a serial mediation model in which crisis leader self-efficacy and motivation to lead during the COVID-19 crisis act as explanatory mechanisms of the relationship between the adaptive personality and the manager's performance. The concept of "continuous improvement" appears straightforward, but it needs a skilled leader to make it work.

How can you create a healthy workplace?

Make sure you have a coherent leadership team, that the leadership team has a common purpose, that you overcommunicate that objective to all employees, and that you reinforce it in all human processes. Traditional leadership training methods appear to take individuals as they are and turn them into leaders by talking to them about leadership concepts and abilities. There is some self-exploration, but my impression is that the the notion of leadership relatively move on rapidly, with less emphasis on self-exploration as a leader. That's not a problem. However, in my opinion, who you are is the most important component in defining the type of leader you will be.

Your training as integrated coaches supports this viewpoint. You strive to figure out who you are and what it entails for your leadership style and decisions. When you engage with your executive customers to help them develop their businesses, When you work with your executive clients to help them become more adaptable leaders, you start by figuring out who they are—what their personality type is, how they handle stress, how they communicate, what they value, and so on. All of this is in the service of gaining a better understanding of themselves as individuals and then implementing the notion of leadership in light of that knowledge.

What can you do to help your organisation become future-ready?

You can focus your attention on the following:

- Promote quick transitions from existing to new technologies that increase value generation (e.g., AI, automation, machine learning).
- Encourage quick and efficient teamwork and coordinated reactions, and eliminate hierarchy and rivalry across different business sectors and levels so that everyone can focus solely on creating value.
- Enable employees to feel the strongest sense of autonomy, mastery, growth, purpose, and connectedness .
- Make significant investments in helping people reach their full potential by employing the most effective techniques for quickly and sustainably enhancing personal capacity.
- The good news is that such organisations do exist and their success determinants are not a secret, even though the percentage of organisations that are genuinely future-fit may be low and awareness of what future-fit implies may be sporadic.

If we are ready to acknowledge that conventional approaches might not be the most effective in a changing environment, we might learn from such innovators. Make it frictionless for brilliant ideas from the front lines to make it through to practical implementation Invest heavily in helping people reach their full potential, using the best techniques to quickly and sustainably build. Throughout the century's relative stability, precedent has frequently served as the foundation for decisions. This usually takes the form of "let's do what we did last time" or "let's do what my boss says" (often based on what worked for them last time). Experience may be a useful instructor, but in modern times, it can be erroneous for two reasons: to begin with, when a new industrial revolution begins, the discontinuities mean that what was successful previously will not be successful again.

If decision-making had been based on precedent, Tesla and Uber would not have existed if decision-making had been based on precedent. Secondly, regardless of IQ, relying on one person's opinion greatly increases the risk of making a poor choice. This is because one is exposed to the unconscious cognitive biases of that person. It is much preferable to consider a variety of viewpoints in an inclusive manner in order to make a choice that is more likely to be solid and shared.

Studies are demonstrating the benefits of diverse teams on decision-making is given below:

- This inclusivity may involve consulting not just a wide range of workers but also consumers and other stakeholders when making the most important choices. That doesn't imply that the choice should come down to a vote or a popularity contest, but it does imply that presumptions should be questioned and different viewpoints should be brought together.
- When making unique decisions, specifically, future-fit organisations take measures to guarantee that the limitations of precedent-based thinking are addressed. They also embrace the value of varied viewpoints.

"As per Gallup findings, when given the option to decide which activities to do, when to complete them, and how much time to devote to each activity, employees are 43% less likely to suffer from severe levels of burnout."

Trust is more fundamental than any other aspect of an organisation's code of ethics. Employees that are trustworthy appreciate the challenge and honor of being a valued part of an organisation's day-to-day struggles and accomplishments. They repay the confidence placed in them by demonstrating their commitment to the organisation when it is most in need.

When everything is up in the air, individuals are stronger when they stick together and help one another in modest steps toward a common goal. These modifications should be led by designated changemakers. Honest debates and even spontaneous exchanges of ideas can aid in the advancement of change. Experiment, test, and record change: It's no secret that in times of significant change, flexible businesses rely on essential individuals they can trust. It takes more than a strong willingness to ride through change to turn it into a consistent, practical model with a roadmap and quantifiable goals.

Clients and stakeholders are frequently concerned that sensitive information may fall into the wrong hands when teams access databases remotely. For major enterprises or even small businesses to contemplate workforce flexibility, additional levels of security in the form of masking, network support, and encryption are essential. Crash courses and hands-on learning, which are typically done alone, provide the vital aspect of adaptation to this massive shift in working and engagement styles. The youthful workforce in India is fearless of change.

"According to a study, 53% of workers would consider changing occupations if it meant more flexibility on the job."

You can sense the difference when you come into a high-performing organisation. People are energised rather than going through the motions. Rather than being puzzled or resigned, they are confident in their organisation's direction and the changes that are taking place. They understand what they are meant to be doing and how it connects to their neighbors' activities. Checking performance measurements like sustained profitability and market share growth at organisations as well as social impact in the charity arena, can swiftly validate your informal findings.

How has the working environment changed in the aftermath of the pandemic?

Adaptive workplaces may become even more appealing in a post-pandemic environment. Employees have a say in where they work, shaping the dialogue, shaping the workplace, and eventually impacting leadership choices, which is a key part of adaptable workplaces. Employees' well-being, passion for the job, and dedication to the organisation are all enhanced when they have a sense of choice and control over when, how, and where they conduct their work. Here are a few instances of workplaces that are adaptable: Siemens has stated that its workers would be able to work two or three days a week from wherever they feel most productive. Employees at Twitter may work from anywhere in the world at any time. With no top-down-driven minimum need for in-office work, most professionals and project teams at Deloitte establish the adaptable working environment that works best for them and their clients.

Improved work/life balance and reduced stress: reports of reduced stress and burnout, as well as increased productivity and more time to focus on family support, as a result of the ability to telework or work remotely, even for one or two days per week. What I feels that working online allows her to be much more attentive to clients, and that saving time on travelling allows her to engage more clients while feeling motivated. Virtual touchpoints approach to virtual communication with families, such as short phone calls or text updates, to help her establish connections in preparation for longer visits and more intensive chats that improved interaction with teenagers and young people.

> "*According to anecdotal evidence, virtual communication channels are especially effective with teenagers and young people.*"

You are enthusiastic about empowering individuals and organisations to thrive in the face of continual and disruptive change, and you accomplish this via programs that address organisational change, resilience, agility, leadership, transformation, and adaptation. Strong organisations are what make the difference for successful businesses.

To make work easier for everyone, your team agreed on which tasks should be done collectively and which should be done separately. The team, for example, decided that planning activities should be done jointly but that targeted activities, such as data analysis, should be done alone. They might organise collaborative activities on their team's co-located days by doing this for a variety of projects. Making virtual watercoolers a possibility: while there is no alternative to face-to-face conversations, there are techniques to replicate comparable, spontaneous encounters in a virtual environment. You and your colleagues use a range of channels to enable seamless collaboration between co-located and remote workers.

Is your organisation agile?

While some organisations may be trying to reinvent themselves, the dangers of transition for businesses with huge and complicated structures are extremely significant. The caterpillar-and-butterfly principle that underpins the promise of sweeping digital transformation does not apply to adaptable organisations. Indeed, in a constantly evolving adaptive mindset, digital change can only be achieved in an evolutionary manner as responses to changing market forces, anticipated or new business opportunities, and emerging risks and threats; and can only be addressed if there is digital agility to pivot when and for what is required. To guide their strategy, these companies must be able to continually monitor market signals, customers, rivals, the value chain, and people.

Digitised situational awareness is assisting organisations in being more adaptable. Situational awareness is not just being aware of current events impacting an organisation but also being able to contextualise those events in the framework of what is expected in order to understand what they mean, as well as being aware of what is likely to occur in the near future.

Situational awareness, in a digital sense, refers to a system of insight that uses all available data pertaining to certain occurrences that must be comprehended holistically and acted upon to achieve the desired change.

Situational awareness is not a new idea, but its use in modern business is rapidly growing. organisations that want to be more nimble might benefit from digitized situational awareness. An agile team's alignment to the customer value stream, as well as its proximity to customer interactions, guarantees that it can continuously sense consumer behavior and give insights to guide the next iteration of a company's market proposal, for example.

Organisations are beginning to leverage their growing volumes of data to produce insights that will help them make better decisions. However, because of the magnitude and complexity of the data, reliable, actionable, and timely information that might provide a competitive edge is difficult to gather.

"An adaptable company that is always monitoring and anticipating changes in its competitive environment requires reliable and accurate information."

Leading companies collect and translate data into easily digestible operational, customer, market, and risk signals on a regular basis. These signals are the analytic building blocks that AI systems employ to increase prediction accuracy in the context of expected outcomes in order to improve situational awareness. In order to accomplish the requisite dynamic agility, the supporting technology must also be digitally agile. IT systems must not only be available everywhere and simple to use, but they must also be easily modified, developed, or replaced to meet new market problems. Situational awareness, real-time signals and insights, and contemporary and adaptable technology all complement and increase the impact of each capacity.

"An organisation that takes this comprehensive strategy will achieve more than it could with just one or two of these talents."

Adaptive businesses prioritise a common vision at all levels of the organisation, with a strong emphasis on delivering value to customers and the broader stakeholder community. These companies have cultures that are engaged, motivated, and high-performing, and they adjust to change quickly and easily. To drive the evolution of its business, an adaptive organisation will constantly analyse and anticipate changes in its market. With an adaptable attitude, these companies respect situational awareness and engage in the design and implementation of digital and data projects to support it. These businesses also utilize data to develop, test, and enhance new value-creating initiatives and business models.

Organisations that haven't evolved and adapted sufficiently throughout time those organisations needed a major wakeup call, and they're either going to receive it now or they won't be around. According to me, this grave prognosis stems in part from the fact that there is no blueprint for this degree of change. .

"Organisations must develop new methods of working and productivity metrics. Such new ways of working need a level of leadership competency that has not previously been highlighted or rewarded."

When faced with a disruption, leaders are put to the test, and they frequently behave in one of two nonproductive ways: others overconfidently apply unexamined know-how rather than adopting an adaptive approach by defining or reframing issues, exploring new domains, and innovating, rather than taking a reactive approach by defining or reframing problems, exploring new domains, and innovating.

Change is happening at a breakneck speed. Three sorts of leaders help an agile organisation adjust fast. The first is the entrepreneurial leaders who come up with innovative goods and business models at a lower level in the organisation. They become the organisation's innovation engine. There are also enabling leaders who assist entrepreneurial leaders in advancing their ideas and communicating strategic imperatives. Architecting leaders, who arc frequently found at the top of an organisation, design the game boards on which entrepreneurial and facilitative leaders operate. They enable people to form teams, access resources for fresh ideas, and continue to develop. They also develop funneling systems to strike a balance between inventive freedom and chaos.

Interestingly, during the pandemic, pharmaceutical corporations were considerably more agile, forming what you term "teams of teams." Most new vaccines and new COVID drugs were developed by corporations that collaborated with regulators, universities, other pharmaceutical companies, and biotech companies. Teams from various organisations were experimenting and breaking down the traditional stages to help propel new goods forward in ways you've never seen before.

Courageous leaders with a long-term view and a commitment to the organisation's future lead adaptive organisations. They have solid talent pipelines and succession strategies in place. Leaders are generally created by participation in and reflection on real-world situations, which are supported by additional training and development activities. Reflection and lifelong learning are ingrained in the culture. Most of today's intractable problems are beyond the knowledge and competence of even the most seasoned professionals.

"Learning is one of the most important qualities in today's environment, and an adaptable organisation is receptive to it."

Front-line perspectives are considered in strategic decision-making; mistakes are not punished; retreats and opportunities to reflect are routine and include a cross-section of the organisation; breakdowns are treated as opportunities to learn; collaboration across all boundaries is encouraged; strategic plans are respected but not treated as sacred and unchangeable texts.

Adaptive organisation necessitates initiatives that engage individuals in your system to address important issues. These interventions have a few characteristics: they forgo fast fixes in favor of long-term solutions; they make people uncomfortable, but they use the discomfort to build traction; they establish and employ new networks of connections; and they improve the organisation's overall adaptive ability.

Slowing down the organisation from moving too quickly and reflecting before acting is often the most useful thing you can do. Ask more questions, withhold your support for a decision until the right time, add extra time to meeting agendas to discuss the adaptive challenge, expand the circle of stakeholders, and separate distracting arguments from the real issues underlying the adaptive issue are some of the useful ways to do this.

How will you reshape, restructured, revamp, and re-establish your organisation?

While an evolution signals a step forward in digital modernisation for certain businesses, protracted and costly transformations may not always provide the expected results. No questions are avoided in highly adaptable organisation, and no subjects are deemed too sensitive to discuss. There is a shared responsibility for the organisation's future. In many ways, adaptive organisations demonstrate a sense of shared responsibility for the whole: they frequently engage in cross-functional problem-solving, people feel free to discuss issues outside their purview at meetings, and the compensation and reward system reflects shared accountability for the company's performance. The ability to make independent decisions is appreciated and anticipated. Managers at the highest levels talk about topics that aren't related to their functional responsibilities. After participating in robust give and take, people may modify their beliefs and attitudes in a free and open debate.

"Now is the moment for businesses to build leaders who can adjust themselves and their organisations to deal with disruptions while doing their daily tasks."

Adaptive businesses The ability of businesses to adjust to changing circumstances is critical. Disruptions can be viewed as a danger, which requires resistance, or as an opportunity, which requires adaptation. According to me, the inclusion of "uncertainty" in the concept of leadership is a plus since it means that one does not have to know all of the answers. In reality, you can't fix it yourself as a leader in an adaptive environment. All you can do is assist your group in making growth, and that is a success. Taking on a variety of challenges you survive by solving challenges that emerge in the lives of your groups, whether it's an organisation, a community, a patient, or an institution.

> "*Adaptability takes us from enduring a difficulty to thriving beyond it, whereas resilience takes us from surviving a challenge to thriving beyond it.*"

You don't simply "bounce back" from adversity; you "bounce ahead" into new realms, learning to be more adaptive as your circumstances change. A multifaceted concept of adaptability includes learning agility, emotional flexibility, and an openness to new experiences. They assist us in maintaining purposeful calm under duress and displaying interest in the face of change. They enable us to respond in ways that are the polar opposite of a knee-jerk reaction by allowing us to make deliberate decisions.

> "*According to a Gartner poll of more than 800 HR professionals, nine HR trends have emerged as a long-term effect of the workforce and workplace changes caused by the coronavirus pandemic disruption. For those executives, the task now is to examine the impact of each HR trend on their organisation's operations and strategic goals, determine which demands immediate action. As a cost-cutting tactic, 32% of companies are replacing full-time staff with contingent labor.*"

Executives C-Suite Calculate and plot business outcomes on a timeline. Describe the technical and interpersonal skills you've developed as a result of your leadership development. Ensure that articulated purpose and talent management executives are enabled by competences. Explain the stages of leadership competency for different types of leaders, such as individual contributors, subject matter experts, project managers, executives, people leaders, high performers, and emerging executives. Incorporate expected outcome delivery into recruiting, onboarding, learning and development, and performance management methods. Ensure that thought leaders' leadership approaches are tailored to your organisation's goals.

Design, develop, and implement leadership development programs that are iteratively designed, developed, and deployed by the leaders who engaged in steps one through three above. Iterate material based on the most important aspirations and intents. Leaders must be re-engaged in order to continue their education. Engage learners in refining learning content as the deployment continues by giving application examples, new application scenarios, and hazards. Baseline indicators of employee engagement and sentiment, such as individual experiences with diversity, equity, and inclusion, job value, leadership quality, and teamwork, are used to assess effects. Adaptive organisations' leadership Roles when members of the C-suite, talent management, people leaders, and individual contributors (such as subject matter experts) who lead without direct reporting and L&D professionals work together, successful programs emerge.

As you've seen, organisations are always confronted with technological and adaptive obstacles. Adaptive challenges provide a more unclear problem to be solved, whereas technical challenges have a well-defined problem that can be solved by professionals. Adaptive leadership as a framework can be a beneficial method to handle such issues. Furthermore, despite the hurdles that come with this strategy, building this skill allows businesses to prosper in the long run. Employees of a phenomenally successful were departing for rivals, despite the fact that they were highly talented and well-trained. Although the organisation generated excellent income, staff turnover began to have a negative impact on the bottom line.

There is currently no playbook available to help firms through the present chaos. Many views, as well as thorough measures, are required to present a more realistic picture of contemporary economic challenges. It is more crucial than ever to have leaders that listen and encourage cooperation. Instead of relying on a top-down strategy to maintain the status quo, this unique period requires transformational leadership, in which management collaborates with employees at all levels to implement critical changes. In this new climate, modest executives are more likely to ensure healthy group dynamics and discover the inspiration needed to propel their company ahead.

> *"According to McKinsey & Company, modest leaders are more likely to succeed."*

Adaptive ability will continue to determine who emerges on top and who goes away in 2022. HR executives can assist corporate leaders in evaluating their default habits and embracing their ability to adjust. The Impact of the Pandemic on Businesses The epidemic shook up the corporate world, especially in terms of how people see leadership, delegation, performance management, and trust. It also prompted concerns regarding remote work productivity, procedures that obstruct existing processes, new health and safety-related job standards, and how to benefit from new production and delivery methods. The ability of businesses to respond to these issues is strongly tied to their executives' ability to adapt.

> *"Many organisations managed to modify their operations models throughout the pandemic, according to McKinsey & Co., with the development of remote work."*

Businesses that had a successful transformation were more likely to perform in the top quartile of their peers. Businesses that did not invest in change, on the other hand, fared the poorest. This just goes to demonstrate that adaptability is the key to future success. It's vital to remember that adaptive capability is a continuum. Some leaders (and organisations) are considered inherently nimble, while others must work hard to improve their adaptability. However, in the long term, the efforts to overcome any barriers will be worthwhile. All HR executives need to do now is get the rest of the organisation on the same page.

> *"According to McKinsey & Co., will maintain momentum and prevent the organisation from becoming exhausted. One of the first duties for anybody trying to design a learning path for teachers is to make sure that the task's scope is appropriate for the amount of time and other resources required to complete it. More disruptive changes, according to HR experts, will backfire."*

HR executives must explain why agility and flexibility are so important for success, and leaders must recognise the need of adaptive capability leadership. Then, and only then, should executives be encouraged to think about the company's operational model. Is it assisting and connecting teams rather than hindering them? Is it going to pave the road for a prosperous future?

The problem is frequently unknown or difficult to define; it is linked to underlying patterns or dynamics and necessitates learning. The remedy is also unknown, necessitating learning. Those who are affected by the challenge (stakeholders), including authorities, have responsibility. The barriers are more intangible: hearts and minds, ideals, loyalty, and connections.

Consider yourself the HR Director of a corporation with a significant turnover rate. Employees that are highly trained and competent are leaving the company for rivals, which has a negative impact on the bottom line.

What strategy would you use to tackle this problem?

If you approach this scenario as a technological problem, you could be inclined to use technical solutions to fix it. Perhaps you require a new incentive scheme to keep your top employees? Perhaps they require more frequent rewards? Perhaps their bosses aren't doing a good job encouraging and engaging them, and they need to improve? You could attempt these remedies and discover that they either don't work or just work for a short period of time.

An adaptive lens may be more successful in solving this problem in the long run. If you think this is an adaptive difficulty, you should spend some time investigating what's going on. The alternative is to lose individuals and miss out on important talent. Employment flexibility 44% was cited as the primary reason for people who briefly left the workforce returning. The importance of flexibility is obvious, and leaders should think about these three aspects of flexibility if they truly want to meet their employees' needs.

Finally, for the development of adaptive leadership a new leadership development framework is required. Employees have a say in where they work, shaping the dialogue, shaping the workplace, and eventually impacting leadership choices, which is a key part of adaptable workplaces. Employees' well-being, passion for the job, and dedication to the firm are all enhanced when they have a sense of choice and control over when, how, and where they conduct their work.

Adaptive ability will continue to determine who emerges on top and who goes away in 2022. HR executives can assist corporate leaders in evaluating their default habits and embracing their ability to adjust. HR analytics benefits firms by assisting them in making proactive decisions that help them mitigate risks and stay on top of things. It may assist in the provision of vital data and the subsequent improvement of spending, productivity, and operations, all of which benefit a business holistically. If you think this is an adaptive difficulty, you should spend some time investigating what's going on. You might enlist the help of your HR department or engage an outside expert to do an objective evaluation of what is pushing your staff to go.

People strategy is as important as business strategy in leading firms. Through people initiatives, the HR department has successfully transformed business strategy into people objectives and supported business priorities. Strategic, functional, and transactional activities are clearly separated within the function. It effectively completes functional and transactional tasks while also influencing strategic issues. Many organisations may need to alter their HR skills to be able to supply line managers with data and advice in order to execute these various jobs and become strategic partners.

To make work easier for everyone, tasks should be done collectively and which should be done separately. The team, for example, decided that planning activities should be done jointly but that targeted activities, such as data analysis, should be done alone. Juan might organise collaborative activities on their team's co-located days by doing this for a variety of projects.

"Organisations that excel in adaptability foster employees' creativity"

Adaptability is a feature that can lead to the development of other desirable attributes in people and organisations. A company that can function effectively in unforeseen conditions can adopt whole new approaches. Such businesses have the technology, manpower, and tools to outperform the competition at any moment. Adaptive organisations are better suited to lead and set the pace for a whole industry.

"You can't build an adaptable organization without adaptable people - and individuals change only when they have to, or when they want to."

Long-term success requires adaptability. It is critical to survive in times like today, when the world is in the grip of a worldwide epidemic. Because they failed to adapt to the ever-changing business landscape, company giants such as

Myspace, Kodak, and RadioShack are now just memories.

Everything in an organisation is influenced by culture. It's just the way things are done here. A culture that encourages individuals to feel psychologically good while also motivating them to achieve peak performance motivates them to be extremely successful. As a consequence, dedication, trust, motivation, kinship, focus, and social involvement characterise the organization and workforce. These are the characteristics and behaviors that make businesses so successful.

- Because capability building is a natural function of an organisation, the goal of leadership is to guide it toward an enabling mission, which leads to vision. For example, Jeff Bezos is well-known for his belief that meetings centred on PowerPoint did not result in increased capability to carry out their mission. As a consequence, he came up with the narrative meeting process.
- You must be intentional and vocal about the importance of learning in your organisation, and you must welcome input from individuals, groups, and the entire organisation. This enables your mental models to be constantly updated to reflect reality, making your organization adaptive, agile, and responsive to both internal and external conditions and events of consequence, increasing your likelihood of market dominance and success significantly more than your competition.
- Leaders must always provide coherence to a continuous improvement process by buffering it from—or linking it to—other imperatives that exist in a district at any given time if it is to thrive. Leaders will encounter conflicting expectations without any buffering or bridging, making

it impossible to produce anything cohesive.

- When the whole organisation supports these cultural norms and practices, the power of adaptation develops. You've discovered a few key factors based on your expertise with both virtual and in-person capability development. Organisations must grab the chance to mix these components with the more conventional in-person immersion experience as they enter a new chapter of hybrid work.

- In actuality, only a small number of leaders are prepared to listen to others who disagree with them. What such leaders fail to realise is that listening does not always imply forsaking one's own objectives. It simply implies that you have a better understanding of your employees' requirements. As a result, you'll be able to work more efficiently to implement modifications.

- Although adaptive leadership demands a significant amount of work, it pays off handsomely. Adaptive businesses, according to trustworthy statistics, reap enormous financial and operational benefits.

- Even during moments of turbulence, they are able to withstand storms and surge to the top. Providing enough time and space for the job helps instructors stay motivated and not feel overwhelmed.

- Building a culture of relational trust allows employees to use the change effort's procedures and structures in ways that are more about learning than performance, and to have open and honest discussions that lead to better practice.

- For the development of adaptive leadership a new leadership development framework is required. One that can be given at scale and creates adaptable leaders at all levels, sooner in their careers and in the flow of their work.

- The new model stresses learning in the context of the organisation's business conditions, processes, and objectives, as well as quick implementation of what has been learned.
- Starting with helping leaders understand the business, including its goals, mission, and goods and services, there are multiple activities and numerous keys to producing adaptable leaders. HR executives must rethink workforce and employee planning, management, performance, and experience methods as the pandemic resets important work patterns.
- Hierarchies must play a supporting role in enabling a constantly evolving network of teams. These groups require adaptable leaders. Leaders who are flexible the way people live, work, and conduct business will continue to be shaped and reshaped by long-term upheaval and change.
- Adaptive organisations must look beyond incremental development and address current practices' flaws on a regular basis.
- Adaptive leaders need to climb up on the roof from time to time to observe what's coming over the horizon. When they detect the potential for disruption, they must move rapidly to plan responses in concert with other leaders.
- Employers must implement flexible work arrangements to enable current living choices, according to younger generations. This applies to both when and where to work.
- Flexible work environments have also been a major success factor in several firms for attracting female professionals and balancing inequity, with enhanced

workplace safety and health records as a side effect. Despite this, most organisations see flexible work environments as a possibility, a fantasy, reserved for the rare Friday-at-home rather than the norm.

- In a turbulent, unpredictable, complicated, and ambiguous environment, a players defined in practice through an iterative, incremental, and emergent delivery strategy becomes a valuable survival weapon.
- Remember that self-organised systems can evolve and enhance their behavior and structure in order to better adapt to changing external situations.
- Predicting trends over the next day, month, quarter, or year is also difficult. Following a meeting with your finance staff, shareholders, and vendors, and with a comprehensive understanding of the company's financial state—including current cash flow, credit situation, income and costs, and so on adapting to change is what makes you useful, relevant, and on the cutting edge of innovation.
- Failure, learning, accountability, and change are all things that an adaptive company embraces.
- Adaptive organisations strive to provide proactive innovation, satisfy consumers and other stakeholders, and lead with appreciation and wisdom in the corporate environment.

> *"Innovative organisations are more adaptable to their surroundings and outperform their competitors."*

Organisations must develop new methods of working and productivity metrics. Such new ways of working need a level of leadership competency that has not previously been highlighted or rewarded. When faced with a disruption, leaders are put to the test, and they frequently behave in one of two nonproductive ways: Others overconfidently apply unexamined know-how rather than adopting an adaptive approach by defining or reframing issues, exploring new domains, and innovating, rather than taking a reactive approach by defining or reframing problems, exploring new domains, and innovating.

An organisation that is nimble is one that adapts quickly to changes in the market and workplace trends. Such businesses recognise that organisational change is unavoidable, so they regularly review their practices and processes to ensure that they are conducive to optimal employee engagement, morale, and performance. An agile organisation responds to new competitors successfully and quickly; they are innovative and are always challenging themselves to advance, respond, and modify.

"Our cancerous corporate mindset stems from a corrupting logic that separates us from and puts us in opposition to our genuine selves, one another, and the outside world. Our faulty philosophical and socio-economic worldview has become ingrained in our everyday consciousness to the point that a large portion of our collective behaviour is conducted under the assumption that this is just the way life is."
- Dr. Amit Das

CHAPTER THREE

Solving The Adaptable Leadership Paradox For Long-Term

"Leadership is lifting a person's vision to high sights, the raising of a person's performance to a higher standard, the building of a personality beyond its normal limitations."
-Peter Drucker

People in every business devise new techniques to escape the unpleasantness of change. Diverting attention away from the problem (e.g., denying the problem exists, focusing on only the technical aspects, creating a surrogate conflict, refusing to consider certain options, using humour to lower the temperature, forming new committees) and displacing responsibility (e.g., blaming/scapegoating others both inside and outside the organisation, marginalising those who have raised the issue) are two of the most common work avoidance strategies.

Keep an eye out for actions that allow people to lower the thermostat and avoid facing the adaptation challenge. Pay close attention, interpret, and intervene as needed. These three abilities are required for adaptive leadership:

- Remark: The goal must be as objective as possible. This is making its way up to the balcony from the dance floor. From this vantage point, you have more distance and a new capacity to view yourself and others in action.
- Representations: Interpretations are inescapable since your brain is built to make sense of things. You must take time to think about how you lead as an adaptable leader. Before you act, interpret what you've seen. Also, pay attention to what you hear and sense that individuals aren't speaking out loud.
- Interventions: The next logical question is what will you do about it after you've seen and reflected on your interpretation? Every intervention is a reaction to your issue hypothesis.

Consider your intervention an experiment aimed at establishing a larger framework that relates your issue interpretation to the adaptive challenge. There's no need to get defensive if the intervention fails if you approach it with an experimental perspective.

You can learn more if you have an exploratory mentality. Be ready to be both perfectly correct and entirely incorrect at the same moment. Whatever you blame for today's tumultuous business climate, an organisation's capacity to weather the storm and adapt is dependent on its people. They may be promised nothing more than the prospect of a brighter future in exchange for these sacrifices. This type of painful organisational transformation is referred to as "adaptive change," which is distinct from the "technical change" that people in positions of power face on a daily basis. While technical issues might be difficult to address, they can be tackled using existing knowledge and the organisation's present problem-solving methods.

Adaptive issues are resistant to these types of solutions because they need employees across the business to change their methods. Because people are the problem, they are also the solution. Short-term appeal may exist in responding to an adaptive problem with a technological remedy. However, in order to achieve genuine progress, it is necessary to act sooner rather than later. Natural disasters, worldwide turmoil, technological advancements, political rules, or economic instability might all be the first domino to fall. They have an impact on customer confidence and expenditure, as well as open the door to new rivals and increase expenses. Many of these drivers are beyond the control of organisations.

Managers and leaders, on the other hand, may prepare themselves to face these challenges and changes. They position their companies to make evolution simpler by tapping into the unique capabilities and expertise of workers at all levels and empowering them. However, encouraging employees at all levels to take responsibility rather than expecting to be given solutions and told what to do may be a significant cultural adjustment for many businesses.

However, we must adopt this entirely new perspective in our interactions with one another. And everyone in the company, at every level, has to be on board. Make room for a flexible leader. For a long time, no one has endorsed command-and-control leadership. However, no completely defined alternative has arisen. This is largely due to high-level executives' apprehension about changing their own habits. They understand that their organisations must become more innovative, and they believe that this will not happen unless they are ready to delegate control, decision-making, and resource allocation to lower levels of the organisation. But they're afraid that if they let go of the reins, the company will implode. An agile organisation adjusts swiftly to an ever-changing environment. I investigate leadership capabilities and antecedents to leadership development.

How businesses might evolve from bureaucracy to become more nimble, agile, learning, and networked?

An agile organisation can swiftly adjust to an ever-changing reality. I used to refer to the world as "VUCCAD," which stands for "volatile, uncertain, complex, critical, ambiguous, and dynamic" but now it's a "VUCCAD" world on steroids. Change is happening at a breakneck speed.

Research shows that organisations with strong cultures that encourage adaptation do better financially than those that don't. In this book, I've explored five measures that leaders can take to become more flexible, including stressing both well-being and purpose, cultivating an adaptive mindset, deepening human relationships, and creating a safe learning environment.

Organisational silos, unclear strategy, and delayed decision-making, according to the CEOs, regularly obstruct initiatives to increase work productivity. Building speedier decision-making systems, boosting internal communication and cooperation, and increasing the number of employees are the three main ways that leaders perceive to solve these obstacles. Executives are supervising a seismic shift in how organisations function as a result of the pandemic, ranging from tactical changes in areas like meeting format and cadence, and day-to-day management, to enterprise-wide changes in leadership and people management, technology use, and innovation.

For most CEOs, creating a future-ready organisation will be a tremendous task. Nobody can accurately forecast the future, nor does anybody have a clear vision of it. Short-term skills and long-term strategic aim must be balanced culturally. In practise, the present serves as a vital source of funding for the future. It is crucial to focus on developing an organisational culture that enables organisations to adapt, crystallise, and execute on plan as the future becomes increasingly obvious before attempting to design long-term strategies for the future.

"Organisations will need to constantly adapt and create an organisational culture that encourages ongoing learning and growth. Success will depend on innovation."

Today, no sector or company is immune to disruption, yet many companies are ill-equipped to adapt rapidly enough to withstand the consequences of rapid change. In the second year of the pandemic, the workplace became a fraught battleground, with employees seeing opportunities to rethink what they wanted out of work and participating in the so-called "great resignation" and employers attempting to define a new normal while COVID-19 and its variants wreaked havoc on even the best-laid plans.

You looked for companies that were either providing the kinds of tools that were designed to create a thriving, positive environment regardless of whether work was done in person, hybrid, or fully remote, or that inherently understood the nature of this tumult and adapted their policies and approaches to serve employees in this charged environment. You are continuously on the lookout for new trends to keep up with. Leaders and entrepreneurs should, however, avoid becoming overawed by the future or the upheaval that is, in large part, being brought about by technology. They have to contribute to co-creating the future.

> *"Technology won't determine the course of history. Geographics shouldn't determine the future. We are here to create our future. We have the ability to create the future we choose."*

Organisations are incorporating sophisticated computer technologies into their organisational processes to enhance efficiency and improve service delivery thanks to the emergence of big data. However, the importance of analytics and big data in innovation within and between enterprises is at the center of this discussion. Most organisations assimilate technology innovation through a complicated, haphazard, top-down approach.

A constant and spontaneous adaption process, on the other hand, may be more natural and increase assimilation quality. It investigates the link between organisational structures and innovation, focusing on a variety of organisational design ideas. It also examines organisational innovation from the micro-level of organisational learning and knowledge generation. It claims that various organisational structures have distinct learning and knowledge patterns. It claims that organisations of various structural forms have varied learning and knowledge generation patterns, resulting in different sorts of inventive capacities.

The debate then focuses to organisational adaptation and transformation, with an emphasis on whether and how companies can overcome inertia in the face of discontinuous technology developments and extreme adjustments in environmental conditions. For many businesses, innovation is a critical source of growth and a significant determinant of competitive advantage. To achieve innovation, many diverse actors must work together, and activities must be integrated across expert roles, knowledge domains, and application contexts. As a result, organisational formation is critical to the innovation process.

> *"People typically want to cling on to the ideals of their culture that have had personal meaning and relevance for them throughout times of transition."*

When dominant cultures are confronted with stressors such as immigration, they are forced to review their beliefs and are frequently forced to do extremely difficult integrative work. You stand for freedom and respect for all people, and your policy does not correspond with what you believe in, says the needed leadership. The refusal of leaders to listen to other people's perspectives is perhaps the biggest obstacle posed by adaptive leadership.

> *"Adaptive leadership, as previously said, is more about cooperation than it is about power."*

Leaders often revert to tried-and-true methods when they require fresh thinking and decisiveness. Five steps can help you flourish in the face of uncertainty by transforming your relationship with it. Shutdowns and supply-chain breaches are common occurrences. Work-from-home, online shopping, and blockchain-based settlements are all possibilities. If it wasn't evident before, the last year has demonstrated that a dynamic and complicated world is throwing up change at a breakneck speed.

Individuals and businesses must be prepared. That does not imply that you should respond to the next issue that comes our way, but rather that you should be ready to confront it when it happens. There is one tool in particular that can assist leaders in doing so.

> *"Adaptability is defined as the ability to learn quickly and effectively in a variety of conditions. It's more of a meta-skill than a skill—learning how to learn and knowing when to put that learner's mind to work."*

You may keep control over uncertainty by becoming aware of and open to change early, before pressures build to the point when changing direction is considerably more difficult, if not impossible. Adaptability, according to my findings, is a vital success component during times of transformation and systemic change. It enables us to learn more quickly and effectively, and it orients us toward the chances rather than the problems that lie ahead.

However, the same circumstances that make adaptation so vital may also cause dread, causing us to fall back on old habits or solutions that worked in the past. The " adaptability paradox " describes how, when you most need to learn and change, you remain with what you know, frequently to the detriment of learning and creativity. Even good things, like getting a promotion or starting a new job, can become bad if you don't keep a learning mentality while you're under pressure.

People, on the other hand, seldom put in the effort to learn and master anything new unless they have a compelling reason to do so. When motivation strikes, it's frequently accompanied by pressure—pressure to avoid failure, for example, or pressure to achieve a high-stakes reward or incentive.

> *"To avoid falling into this trap, leaders must concentrate on changing their attitudes about change and uncertainty by cultivating flexibility as a lifelong talent that helps both themselves and their businesses. Even for the most successful among us, this is not a natural ability, but it can be developed."*

People who are weary have a scarcity mindset (they focus on what they don't have) and are less adaptive and receptive to learning. These mental-health and well-being issues are likely to persist for at least the next year or two. The greatest method for dealing with difficult conditions is to first invest in one's own well-being. Leaders must be healthy to confront whatever comes their way and to assist others for as long as it takes, just like athletes who invest in their physical and mental health on a regular basis, not just before a game or a race. Leaders should prioritise enabling themselves to grow before assisting others in reaching their full physical, mental, and emotional potential.

Another research found that persons who took breaks to mentally reset improved far more quickly under pressure when doing a job that required new abilities. Attending to one's own physical well-being is not selfish, contrary to what some leaders believe. Rather, good physical and mental health are required to develop strong decision-making abilities in the face of ambiguity. Many executives believe they must demonstrate to their organisations that they are constantly on, never being away of the office for lengthy periods of time or taking necessary vacations. One adversary of the adaptable mentality for leaders is the assumption that it is their role to know when to ask the correct questions rather than having the "perfect answers."

"Leaders who relinquish their expert status might better manage unpredictable situations by gathering data in novel and effective ways. Leaders may demonstrate flexibility in finding answers by adjusting their mentality to foster learning, curiosity, and willingness to change."

Another significant adaptive problem is finding the correct location, time, and rhythms for cooperation. While those at the top may be enthusiastic about collaborative work, instructors may find that their own preparation time is limited or interrupted by meetings.

According to research, adaptability has also been connected to essential psychological abilities such as coping and personal growth. Higher degrees of flexibility in the workplace are linked to increased learning capacity, improved performance, confidence, and creative output.

"Adaptability is also associated with better levels of social support and general life satisfaction, which are important for psychological and physical well-being."

Let's look at five ways leaders may invest in flexibility to prepare for a fast-paced and uncertain future now that you've covered the benefits. Executives have been checking on workers' health since the onset of the COVID-19 outbreak. But it may have been putting the wagon before the horse: a study suggests that leaders suffered from anxiety and burnout symptoms at previously unheard-of levels as they concentrated on others rather than recharging their own batteries.

In the fall of 2020, a Harvard Business Review–sponsored poll garnered comments from over 1,500 respondents from 46 countries, the majority of whom were at or above the supervisor level. 85% claimed their well-being had deteriorated, while 56% said their job obligations had worsened. Furthermore, 62% of those who were having trouble managing their workloads stated they had burned out "often" or "veryfrequently" in the preceding three months. Since then, the number of workers experiencing higher burnout symptoms has risen across the board, not only in C-suites.

CEOs are afraid that their leaders will be unprepared to deal with expected challenges. They also desire greater results from their leadership development efforts. That entails creating adaptive leadership skills and providing them at an organisational level for the chief learning officer (CLO) and learning and development (L & D) professionals.

For example, when burnout rates climbed, C-suite leaders of a global firm struggled with how to effectively support employees during the epidemic. The CEO, as a follower of the "expert attitude," believed he should already know the answers and couldn't tolerate the ambiguity.

> *"Awareness of your default thoughts, knowing when they aren't benefiting you, opening up to what else could be true, and consciously moving into new, flexible thinking are all necessary steps in such a journey."*

Adaptability relies heavily on self-awareness and reflection. Making a to be list—that is, a list of the values You wish to embody—and setting your intentions in the morning, before a hectic day, or at work when things get hard, are two ways to enhance awareness. Reflecting about challenging times at the end of the day aids in the development of a flexible unlocking mentality for the future. The essential problem is not whether you experience fear or uncertainty—you will—but whether you respond to those pressures in ways that cause us to do more of the same instead of learning and changing.

Increase the variety and depth of your connections. Human beings require meaningful connections to survive and develop; therefore, strong interpersonal interactions help them adapt. According to studies, these social networks can have an impact on one's lifespan. You normally go about your everyday work routines, actively doing things and indirectly collaborating with coworkers to complete those tasks. But that emphasis is misplaced: failing to pay attention to colleagues is really harmful to your health and productivity at work. Deep and diversified social ties that give social support, according to research, are essential aspects of the complex tapestry that feeds your well-being and learning, especially during times of uncertainty and heightened stress.

There are a few things you can do as a leader to help people form stronger bonds: concentrate entirely on the person in front of you. You frequently allow your attention to wander during conversations, or you multitask by checking our phone or email. Tuning your consciousness toward the other person and listening carefully and without judgment is required for full attention. People can hear you when they feel heard. Be willing to be vulnerable. Bring your true self to the table and be open to expressing your worries, anxieties, and flaws. While being exposed might seem dangerous, it is always a conscious decision. Empathy is important, but don't stop there. Empathy is insufficient on its own.

Leaders may learn to harness the correct type of empathy, which entails considering the other person's point of view without becoming distracted from the matter at hand or, perhaps, wasting their own energy on negative emotions. Once you've grasped the other person's viewpoint, you'll be able to choose the best course of action. Approach others with empathy. If you see someone else's distress, whether physical, emotional, or social, show that you want to help. Simultaneously, bear in mind that you'll never entirely comprehend what they're going through, so have an open mind. While random acts of kindness are appreciated, compassion is more subtle and tailored to an individual's needs. Adaptability is aided by positive team dynamics. Working in groups has an impact on how you prioritize learning, particularly from setbacks and mistakes.

Why is it so crucial to develop an adaptation muscle?

During the COVID-19 crisis, the strength of resilience was vividly proved. Although resilience and adaptation are closely related, they differ in key ways. Leadership barriers to adaptive capacity changing one's conduct in reaction to adversity does not come easily for many business executives. While most business executives are competent and clever, it can be challenging to acquire new behavioral reactions when their previous habits match their businesses' goals in the majority of circumstances.

Introducing new behavioral options is typically unsettling, and it may make leaders feel exposed. People tend to cling to practices that have served them well in the past, which might limit their ability to change. Rather than waiting for agility to spread from the bottom up, HR executives must support and assist leaders in taking command of their transitions. These techniques can aid in the development of an adaptable leadership style.

The lack of confrontation and the appearance of conformity, on the other hand, may not represent that dynamic. Teams can have cultures in which setbacks and failures are ignored or, worse, penalised, or cultures in which setbacks are viewed as chances to learn and improve.

"Leaders may have a significant impact on the team culture that is established based on how well they nurture psychological safety."

This is a team-wide notion that taking interpersonal risks is safe—that ideas, questions, worries, and blunders will be embraced and encouraged. Experiencing safety is a necessary component of enhanced performance, creativity, and well-being. It encourages everyone to participate fully and authentically, promotes healthy discussion and innovative problem solutions, and helps teams to learn rapidly.

Leaders must be aware of and model the required behaviors, as well as intentionally assist team members, for such an environment to succeed. Simply put, by establishing psychological safety, leaders demonstrate their own adaptability while also fostering an atmosphere in which their people may thrive. This is in stark contrast to a leader who feels, "I am the best", and the team should follow me. The new CEO chose to embark on a journey with this team in order to turn that difficult past into a tale of optimism and opportunity. He enlisted the support of outside coaches to promote team learning, feedback, curiosity, and transformational attitudes. Despite hiccups in the path, the group evolved from a collection of individuals lacking mutual trust to a close-knit team that is much stronger today. Because of the CEO's focus on creating trust, as well as his development mentality and willingness to look vulnerable, a new culture of psychological safety was able to emerge.

Adaptable organisations minimise superfluous hierarchy by devolving governance and decision-making authority to lower levels. When an organisation uses self-organising, cross-functional teams and has a flexible organisational structure that allows employees to easily move between positions and into quickly morphing team structures, performance, innovation, and responsiveness to change all improve.

Sharing authority, prioritising employee needs, and assisting individuals in developing and performing at their best are all important aspects. Adaptive organisational cultures thrive when leaders provide context, eliminate obstacles, and include team members in strategic choices that affect them.

> "*A successful adaptive organisation strives to foster justice, constructive conflict, and psychological safety, which fosters trust, shared accountability, variety of opinion, and risk tolerance.*"

These organisations' employees are free to express their honest opinions about the business climate and how they feel it will affect the company. An adaptable organisation's capacity to grab opportunities as they come – and often even before they arise – is a critical trait. Adoption of technology to modernise and enhance processes, as well as new methods of thinking and working, is required to succeed in these traits. In order to get the competitive advantage that comes with being adaptable, a company is more likely to go through a series of digital evolutions rather than a single transformation.

Businesses should consider the future as a continuum rather than a binary decision between onsite and virtual. Instead, they should seek to establish flexible, adaptable workplaces where people and teams may move about as required, depending on the nature of the job and where they and their teams are most effective. The first step is to distinguish between the dissatisfied now that your organisation was created to solve and the ideal future that it strives to achieve. This aim requires clarity and consensus. It has to be a common mental model. Second, this future aim or state must be intrinsically motivating, serving as a source of inspiration and ambition for everyone in the company throughout both normal and difficult times. Third, visions work best when they are brief and straightforward.

> *"A complicated paragraph is unlikely to inspire, and it is more likely to include empty words or jargon exclusive to one's industry that everyone is sick of hearing."*

Fourth, the vision should be quantifiable. This planned future state must be specific enough that a statistic or metrics can tell you when and if you've arrived. Microsoft's initial ambition was to have "a computer on every desk and in every household." The most significant mental model of every organisation is its vision, which is the intended objective or future state that the company wants.

Organisations must develop new methods of working and productivity metrics. Such new ways of working need a level of leadership competency that has not previously been highlighted or rewarded. When faced with disruption, leaders are put to the test, and they frequently respond in one of two ways: some perceive danger and shut down, while others apply unquestioned know-how rather than taking an adaptive approach by defining or reframing challenges, exploring new domains, and creating.

There are countless examples of once-dominant businesses that failed to sustain their supremacy owing to their failure to adapt to changing circumstances. Consider the case of Kodak. The firm, which was once dominant owing to its photographic films, was sluggish in adapting to digital photography and had to sell many of its patents to stay afloat. Organisations that seek to prevent a similar fate should use the adaptive leadership approach.

> *"According to Darwin's Origin of Species, the species that survives is the one that can adapt and adjust to the changing environment in which it finds itself, not the most intelligent or the strongest."*

While the above remark relates to the significance of adaptability for a species' existence, companies must also be able to adapt to changing conditions. Technical problems might be difficult to address, but they always present a clear problem that can be handled using current knowledge and the experience of a few experts. For example, if your computer isn't working properly, you may have a professional from your company's IT department fix it for you. Adaptive problems, on the other hand, lack a clearly defined problem and necessitate solutions that are outside of the organisation's present competence and know-how.

If an organisation is repeatedly confronted with the same type of crisis, for example, it is most likely experiencing adaptation difficulties. Adaptive leadership is based on four key ideas, which we've mentioned here. Organisational fairness adaptive issues, as previously said, rarely have a clear problem and solution. As a result, fixing them necessitates imagination and inventiveness. As a result, it is critical for an adaptable leader to foster an environment in which all views and opinions are heard. Not only does this result in more innovative ideas, but being a part of the change process also helps individuals feel appreciated. This results in a higher level of buy-in, which is necessary for the solution to be implemented successfully.

Today, Disney is one of the world's greatest media giants, yet it all started with humble origins. Since 1923, Disney has been capturing the imaginations of youngsters and families alike since 1923. Keeping a captivated audience, on the other hand, is no simple task. When the popularity of cult classics such as Donald Duck and Mickey Mouse began to wane, Disney reinvented itself time and again. Take, for example, the latest surge of live-action films that are bringing old favorites like Beauty and the Beast, The Jungle Book, and the much-anticipated Aladdin back to life. Disney's ability to adapt and change with the times while remaining true to its beginnings as a maker of timeless, iconic characters has been critical to its success. To stay relevant, Disney has bought Pixar Studios (in 2006 for $7.4 billion), Marvel (in 2009 for $6 billion), Star Wars

(Lucasfilm in 2012 for $4 billion), and practically all of 21st Century Fox (external link) for $52 billion in shares.

Who could have predicted that Jeff Bezos' concept for an online bookshop, which he launched in his basement in Seattle in 1994, would become the world's largest internet retailer? Amazon has taken the globe by storm, and it all began with a product advertised as "the world's largest book shop." Since then, the internet behemoth has irreversibly altered our consumption habits. Is it possible to get fresh meals via the internet? Done. Same-day or even same-hour delivery? Absolutely.

Amazon has redefined convenience and will continue to do so - Bezos sends out the identical 1997 Annual Report letter to shareholders, emphasising a constant focus on 'obsessing over consumers' and a determination to make daring rather than cautious decisions. The Swedish startup, which was founded in 2008, has revolutionised the way music is delivered and enjoyed in an amazingly short amount of time. Spotify's streaming service, which has 70 million subscribers, has done the unthinkable: it has gotten people to pay for music again. Global revenues soared last year to an estimated $10.8bn, but with Spotify paying out a huge portion of its revenue to the music industry, largely in royalties, how will it move forward without losing money?

Last year's global sales surged to an estimated $10.8 billion, but how can Spotify continue to make money if it pays a major portion of its earnings to the music business, mostly in royalties? Could Spotify be on the verge of disrupting the music industry once more, following in the footsteps of Netflix? Could it try to start its own music label to develop original content rather than pay fees for record rights?

Kodak was formerly the most well-known and groundbreaking name in the world of photography and filmmaking. The firm was instrumental in the development of cameras that were portable, inexpensive, transportable, and eventually affordable for the average person. However, with the development of the digital camera in 1975, Kodak failed to react to technological changes. Remember when anything was referred to as a "Kodak moment"? Kodak controlled the photographic business and was once associated with snapping a picture.

However, the organisation filed for bankruptcy in 2013 because of its failure to adapt quickly enough to the introduction of digital photography, which rendered camera film useless for all but the most ardent traditionalists. The increase followed Kodak's announcement that it would establish its own cryptocurrency, KodakCoin. KodakCoin is a cryptocurrency aimed at photographers that is part of a larger blockchain ecosystem dedicated to safeguarding photographers and giving them control over their image rights. Could Kodak demonstrate that the "Kodak moment" can be resurrected by taking a proactive approach to new technology? The organisation has always held the notion that a printed picture will continue to be valued and appreciated by clients above a digital image.

Of course, they were mistaken, but it was too late to recover their losses by the time they stopped selling classic film cameras in 2004. Since declaring bankruptcy in 2012, Kodak has been striving to reinvent itself. In an unusual turn of events, the business secured a $765 million federal loan in 2020 from the Trump administration to create 25% of the active components for generic pharmaceuticals in the US.

Dialpad, the device-agnostic cloud communications platform, had a strong year in 2021, thanks to the debut of its videoconferencing product, Dialpad Meetings, and text and voice collaboration tool, Dialpad Channels. The company's voice intelligence solution, codenamed Vi, employs AI to assist employees with preserving meeting takeaways or addressing issues that arise during, say, contact between a client and a customer support person.

Dialpad, which was founded by a number of former Google Voice employees, now aspires to be the only communications tool a company needs, whether for videoconferencing, audio conversations, or internal messaging. Hundreds of companies use the software-as-a-service concept to access the company's communications tools.

Hundreds of organisations aiming to streamline and simplify in a remote-first world use the privately held company's communications capabilities via a software-as-a-service approach. Among its publicly traded enterprise customers are Classpass, PagerDuty, ServiceFirst, TED, and Toast.

Who didn't have a Yellow Pages copy next to the phone? The legendary journal was once a lifeline for families all around the United Kingdom. For more than 50 years, the telephone directory has provided clients with business names, phone numbers, and addresses. Given the fast rise of digital and social media, CEO Richard Hanscott declared in 2017 that the firm would discontinue printing in 2019 and transition to digitising its entire operation.

Since the company's inception in 1966, Hanscott has changed the business strategy while maintaining the integrity of the Yellow Pages by offering the same service to clients. It may feel strange not to possess a physical copy, but Yell.com offers the same service, just faster and better.

"The greatest approach to inspiring invention is to foster a culture of thanks and appreciation."

The ability of a company to innovate is a prerequisite for the effective use of innovative resources and new technology. On the other hand, the introduction of new technology frequently confronts businesses with significant possibilities and problems, resulting in changes in management practices and the formation of new organisational structures. Organisational and technical advancements are inextricably linked.

How many organisations are aware of who they are, what they stand for, what drives them forward, and why they are successful?

According to a Chinese saying, many people construct bunkers during strong winds, while others construct windmills. Entrepreneurs will need to choose whether they want to construct bunkers or take advantage of the chance to construct windmills since we are living in a period of great winds and organisations. Employers, legislators, government employees, and society at large face major issues as a result of the disruption that digital technologies are bringing to the workplace.

As we move into the digital age, rapidly developing technologies—like artificial intelligence, machine learning, deep learning, internet of things, automation, blockchain, big data, wearables, robotics, and industry 4.0—are encouraging the creation of new production methods, business models, and value chains that will fundamentally alter the business landscape. The complexity of leading the ship of the future is increased by the pace and breadth of change for leaders and entrepreneurs.

As practice, use bite-size training. Deeper awareness and habit-shifting work were thought to be only possible through intensive in-person interactions, according to popular thinking. The COVID-19 pandemic, like so many other paradigms, shifted that viewpoint. Many companies have implemented brief digital training courses along with behavioral-reinforcement techniques like nudges. This material focuses on teaching fundamental adaptation ideas that participants may apply in their daily lives to help them learn and modify their behaviors more quickly. This method has proven to be beneficial to businesses in transition, such as a worldwide corporation that underwent a difficult merger before the pandemic struck.

Adaptability to changing circumstances is a must-have attribute for today's businesses, especially in this unpredictable environment. Adaptability is a must-have organisational attribute for business executives. There is no assurance that the biggest and fiercest industry incumbents will survive as disruption intensifies. Adaptiveness is built on innovation, and encouraging individuals to think outside the box is critical to achieving it. In every case, these companies have shown an exceptional capacity to adjust swiftly to shifting circumstances. These businesses are well positioned to succeed in unpredictable times, both now and in the future, with the correct strategy and grit.

Many factors will influence an organisation's future health, including changes based on area, industry, and even company type. To keep fit while acquiring dynamic competitive advantages, the unifying thread is to focus on revolutionary business drivers. Consider the human dimension while building business models, products, and services for all company stakeholders. Encourage innovation by researching new ideas ahead of time and supporting innovative corporate cultures. Develop a solid digital transformation plan to keep up with technological improvements and to stay ahead of any possible disruption. Any flexible and future-ready company will have these characteristics. This preparation will allow companies to respond more swiftly to changes in client needs, technological developments, and disturbing competition than companies that rely solely on size and efficiency.

Many other internal and external factors may limit a company's capacity to adapt, but greater planning and transformation may serve as a roadmap for executives wishing to avoid the same blunders that have brought other businesses to their knees. The list of brick-and-mortar companies having to compete against more nimble online competitors continues to expand, from Toys R Us to Austin Reed to HMV.

What about the organisations that were not able to adapt?

Here are top picks for companies that have stayed relevant, predicted trends, and embraced innovation. Do you recall the days when you could rent DVDs? Netflix was founded in 1997 by CEO Reed Hastings and began by shipping DVDs to consumers. It's difficult to fathom without viewing video on demand now that there are over 109 million customers globally. Hastings had the idea in 2001 to transmit movies directly to our televisions over the internet. He experimented for several years to get clients used to streaming rather than watching actual DVDs. Hastings has always dreamed big, but he started small, failed swiftly, and grew rapidly. Netflix has perfected the disruptive innovator's art, producing and authoring its own original blockbuster blockbusters in addition to those created by others. Netflix, which now ranks alongside Facebook, Amazon, and Google as one of the world's leading tech innovators, has revolutionised the way you consume entertainment. Has it broken ties with traditional television networks? What about the big screen's chances of surviving?

> *"Starbucks was founded around the experience and the environment of their stores. Starbucks was about a space with comfortable chairs, lots of power outlets, tables and desks at which we could work and the option to spend as much time in their stores as we wanted without any pressure to buy. The coffee was incidental."*

Yahoo was founded in 1994 and immediately rose to prominence as the go-to site for email, news, and online searches. The downfall of the corporation was caused by a series of poor business decisions. For example, Yahoo missed out on a $1 billion deal to purchase Google in 2002, and then a $1.1 billion deal to buy Facebook in 2006. Yahoo has also been chastised for mismanaging Flickr and Tumblr, failing to prioritize the hiring of high-calibre programming talent, and a leadership team that lacks direction. Yahoo was sold to Verizon in 2016 for just $4.8 billion after a number of failures. In comparison, at its height in 2000, the corporation was valued at $125 billion. Yahoo was the most-read news and media website in 2016, with over 7 billion monthly views, making it the world's sixth most visited website. They controlled 21% of the internet advertising industry in 2005, indicating that they were the market leaders. In 2011, Yahoo's email service had 281 million subscribers, making it the world's third-largest provider of web-based email services.

Facebook entered the arena with a superior user experience and the capacity to connect people via more than simply music, which is what MySpace essentially became as bands and musicians uploaded their songs and mixtapes nonstop. Through Facebook, users were able to connect with current and former friends who had the same hobbies and interests.

Their demise was due to poor management of their expansion. They were already number one, but in order to achieve their goal of becoming an internet gateway, they decided to outsource their search engine to Microsoft Bing. When Yahoo had the opportunity to purchase Google for $5 billion in 2002, they turned it down. In 2006, Yahoo had a contract to acquire Facebook for $1 billion, but the offer was lowered, prompting Mark Zuckerberg to pull out. As of March 22, 2018, Facebook's stock price was $163 billion. Yahoo is currently ranked fourth among the largest internet marketers, a position they are fighting to keep.

Look at this, another camera supplier. In 1991, Polaroid's instant film and cameras helped the company reach a sales record of $3 billion. They possessed the patent on their instant photography method, making them the most well-known names associated with the procedure, which they are still referred to today. Organisations that are unable or unwilling to adapt to disruption, technology improvements, and changing consumer needs have been demonstrated time and time again to fail in the long run. Seven businesses have learnt this lesson the hard way.

Nokia was previously recognized for being incredibly adaptable and forward-thinking, so its downfall was unexpected. In 1996, the business made a significant investment in research and development and created the first smartphone. Nokia, on the other hand, failed to see the importance of software, especially applications, and miscalculated the quick move to smartphones in the years that followed. Nokia, for example, made more than half of its revenue in 2007.

Nokia, for example, made more than half of all earnings in the mobile phone market in 2007, yet the majority of those revenues did not come from smartphones. Apple, on the other hand, was devoting equal attention to both hardware and software development and was well ahead of the curve when it came to smartphone advances. Nokia had only 3% of the worldwide smartphone market by 2013, and it sold its handset division to Microsoft for $7.2 billion in August of that year. Another camera company has gone out of business because they underestimated the impact that digital cameras would have. Polaroid Corporation went bankrupt in 2001, just a decade after earning its highest-ever single-year revenue.

Xerox established the Xerox Palo Alto Research Center (also known as Xerox PARC) in 1970 to explore future technologies. Laser printers, Ethernet, and a forerunner to the modern PC were all developed at the Xerox PARC. However, despite investing substantially in research and development and producing several groundbreaking technologies, the firm struggled to capitalize on market potential and achieve commercial success, ultimately losing out to a corporation with a stronger brand and a far larger ambition. In 1958, Xerox introduced the Xerox 914 photocopier, which revolutionized document printing. It is widely regarded as the most successful single product in history, generating $60 million in sales for Xerox in only three years and rising to nearly $500 million by 1965. Despite having invented the graphical user interface (GUI) and a commercial version of the mouse, when the Macintosh computer was released in 1984, it was Steve Jobs and Apple that realized the benefits of these technologies. Xerox was ultimately unable to capitalize on its ideas and inventions in order to operate a viable, commercial corporation.

Xerox's dilemma was that their own inventions were spurned by their own directors, which led to its demise. Xerox researchers and engineers pioneered a number of aspects of personal computing, but the company's board of directors ordered the engineers to share their discoveries with Apple personnel.These innovations were later taken by Apple and Microsoft, who went on to become the two most powerful computing companies, leaving Xerox in the dust.

"Innovative organisations are more adaptable to their surroundings and outperform their competitors."

Blockbuster is a company that rents out movies and video games. At its peak, Blockbuster had over 9,000 locations worldwide and employed 84,000 people.They were head and shoulders above most other rental outlets in terms of the number and range of titles. Blockbuster's economic model needed to evolve in response to the emergence of Netflix and on-demand streaming, but it did not. Blockbuster did not adapt to the times by adopting a trend that would eventually lead to its demise.

After the merger of Houston Natural Gas and InterNorth, Enron was formed as an American energy, commodities, and service corporation. Enron had 20,000 employees and was one of the world's largest energy, natural gas, and communications corporations. For the sixth year in a row, Fortune magazine named it America's most innovative corporation. Enron's collapse occurred after a scandal showed that the business was plagued with fraud and wrongdoing. To hide dishonesty in their accounting information, they employed a range of misleading and fraudulent accounting methods and strategies. They were essentially misrepresenting any expected or possible earnings from any asset as reality when they weren't (more can be read on that here).

There were once 80 million Blackberry users around the world, including former US President Barack Obama, who stopped using his in 2016. In the mid-to late-2000s, Blackberry Messenger was the dominant form of professional and personal contact, with everyone demanding to know your pin. In a nutshell, the iPhone is doomed. Apple began to dominate the mobile industry by supporting Bring Your Own Device (BYOD) rules and guidelines within organisations, whereas Blackberry disregarded touch-screen-based technologies. In 2014, three years after Apple had incorporated Siri into all of their devices, there were rumors that Blackberry was working on a Siri-like voice assistant named Blackberry Assistant. Blackberry's failure to innovate resulted in their demise.

Because of their inability to innovate, Blackberry quickly fell to a 0.2 percent market share by early 2016. Kodak was the market leader in photographic film during the twentieth century, having been founded in 1888. They came up with the "Kodak moment" phrase, which was used everywhere, and they even got a shout-out from Pitbull in his single "Give Me Everything." Kodak's demise was due to their fear of innovation. They built the first digital camera in 1975, but abandoned it owing to concerns that it would suffocate their photographic film juggernaut. After that, digital seized over, and Kodak's competitors, notably Fuji, outlasted the erstwhile photo monarchs. In 2012, Kodak declared bankruptcy, then resurfaced in 2013, substantially smaller and focused on business clients.

Amazon's innovation engine, which spends $16 billion a year (almost 12% of sales) on "technology and content," with much of it going to IT-related R&D. According to Gartner, retail and wholesale organisations spend significantly less on IT than retail and wholesale organisations, spending only about 1.5 percent of sales on IT. Too many businesses either underinvest in innovative ideas or abandon them too soon. The most adaptable businesses recognise and develop their own innovations and disruption prospects. They invest for the long term by investing in a methodical manner. They take the long view by investing methodically in ideas that may not produce fruit for years (or ever), but when they do, the results might be extremely disruptive. Creating self-organising teams digital efforts generally span numerous departments within a company, and they are unlikely to succeed if departmental barriers get in the way. Many cross-functional SWAT teams with decentralized decision-making and the authority to make quick, day-to-day choices inside their group are needed by companies.

When a company is forced to modify or adapt, it can prosper. Take the bull by the horns and lead the market towards the next iPhone or Google. However, some people are unaware that in order to be successful, they must welcome change. It's critical to acquire some crucial business skills, whether you own a firm or work in a department where you're responsible for a particular amount of duty and accountability. You provide a variety of online and virtual classroom training courses to assist you in filling up any gaps. Before you get started, if you're thinking about changing careers, You've put together a list of resources for you:They may have failed to adapt, but that does not imply they are no longer in business. Keep an eye out to see whether any of the ones you recall are still in operation today.

However, once the iPhone and Android were released, the game was over. Despite its historic purchase of Nokia's phone company, Microsoft has slowly lost market share since then and is now a tiny player in what is perhaps the most significant area of technology. Too many businesses maintain their holy cows, allocating and allocating resources to the same priority year after year in order to ensure that everyone receives their 2% to 3% raise. Instead of sticking to the financial calendar, the most effective leadership teams can unleash funds and resources to put behind crucial new projects when strategic needs change. Amazon's acquisition of Whole Foods threw the retail industry's assumptions into disarray. Grocers have long thought that the food industry is immune to disruption, which has led to a delay in investing in omnichannel solutions.

Take chances and prioritise new ideas by allowing teams to handle challenges together and giving them full ownership of choices; and focus the right people on the right objectives using qualitative and quantitative tools instead of waiting for annual planning sessions. Strategic planning methods that are unable to adjust rapidly enough to market developments and the actions of competitors might have unfavorable outcomes. Consider Microsoft's smartphone experience. It's hard to believe now, but prior to 2007, Windows Mobile 6 was the mobile market leader, with a 30% share over Palm, BlackBerry, and Symbian.

A constant and spontaneous adaption process may be more natural and increase assimilation quality. It investigates the link between organisational structures and innovation, focusing on a variety of organsational design ideas. The ability of a company to innovate is a prerequisite for the effective use of innovative resources and new technology. Many businesses went remote during the worst of the epidemic and have since resorted to a hybrid structure or have brought staff back full-time without much thought. When a company is forced to modify or adapt, it can prosper. Take the bull by the horns and lead the market towards the next iPhone or Google.

When you're done altering, you're done. Maybe it's just a matter of not being too attached to the past. Google is largely regarded as one of the world's most agile and inventive businesses. That isn't to say it hasn't had its share of big-company organisational problems. The alphabet, for example, was created by it. When it put its well-established companies (Google, Gmail, YouTube, Android, and Maps) with Google and its more speculative businesses (Calico, Waymo, Nest, Google Fiber, GV, and CapitalG) with Alphabet, the corporation set out to compete more effectively in the face of continual change.

The goal was to isolate the company's more established money earners from its expansion plans. The new structure would offer each company the freedom to make decisions based on the specifics of its market while avoiding the resource fights that stymie other huge technological organisations. Google established a more flexible organisation that could act depending on the imperatives of each individual business rather than forcing strategic judgments about where to play in a static, function-driven organisation and team structure. An adaptable company has this mindset—namely, the ability to apply inner-game agility to operations, planning, and people management.

Are businesses prepared for what lies ahead as technology continues to transform how people live, work, and lead?

Many organisations are unprepared to make strategic decisions and produce results quickly in this era of constant change. This book, which is based on more than ten years of research, demonstrates that achieving desirable futures calls for an integrated set of methods for identifying, assessing, and responding to change at a rate that is consistent with the environment in which the organisation operates. An organisation is better equipped to steer desirable futures if it can develop advantages in foresight, innovation, and transformation (FIT). The book also demonstrates how future fitness promotes improved organisational performance.

> *"It will be difficult for leaders to meet and adjust to the shifting needs of the future. They will need to make sure that their companies can navigate these choppy waters while still managing to stay afloat."*

Adaptive ability will continue to determine who emerges on top and who goes away in 2022. HR executives can assist corporate leaders in evaluating their default habits and embracing their ability to adjust. The Impact of the pandemic on businesses.

The epidemic shook up the corporate world, especially in terms of how people see leadership, delegation, performance management, and trust. It also prompted concerns regarding remote work productivity, procedures that obstruct existing processes, new health and safety-related job standards, and how to benefit from new production and delivery methods. The ability of businesses to respond to these issues is strongly tied to their executives' ability to adapt.

Many organisations managed to modify their operations models throughout the pandemic, according to McKinsey & Co., with the development of remote work. Businesses that had a successful transformation were more likely to perform in the top quartile of their peers.

Businesses that did not invest in change, on the other hand, fared the poorest. This just goes to demonstrate that adaptability is the key to future success. It's vital to remember that adaptive capability is a continuum. Some leaders (and organisations) are considered inherently nimble, while others must work hard to improve their adaptability. However, in the long term, the efforts to overcome any barriers will be worthwhile. All HR executives need to do now is get the rest of the firm on the same page.

HR executives must explain why agility and flexibility are so important for success, and leaders must recognize the need of adaptive capability leadership. Then, and only then, should executives be encouraged to think about the company's operational model. Is it assisting and connecting teams rather than hindering them? Is it going to pave the road for a prosperous future?

One of the first duties for anybody trying to design a learning path for teachers is to make sure that the task's scope is appropriate for the amount of time and other resources required to complete it. More disruptive changes, according to HR experts, will backfire. The problem is frequently unknown or difficult to define; it is linked to underlying patterns or dynamics and necessitates learning. The remedy is also unknown, necessitating learning. Those who are affected by the challenge (stakeholders), including authorities, have responsibility. The barriers are more intangible: hearts and minds, ideals, loyalty, and connections. Adaptive difficulties are the most difficult because leadership techniques.

But in the quick-changing world of today, "knowing" is no longer relevant. Because market dynamics, technology, legislation, and competition change so fast, historical knowledge is becoming less and less significant. It could result in arrogance and complacency. It could even be harmful at times. In reality, learning is a given in today's rapidly evolving world. It is now a matter of survival rather than merely separating the exceptional from excellent businesses.

You are definitely setting yourself up for failure in the long term if you don't step outside of your comfort zone to try something new, feel awkward, or even fail. Both businesses and their executives may attest to this. You can carry on doing the things that got you where you are now. Like Nokia, you can even get pretty excellent at it.

However, the competition keeps modifying the game's regulations while you are still improving yourself, making it harder for you to catch up with the competition.

How can you create a future-fit healthy workplace?

Make sure you have a coherent leadership team, that the leadership team has a common purpose, that you overcommunicate that objective to all employees, and that you reinforce it in all human processes. This ushered in a new age for business, one in which the ability to adapt is crucial to existence.

Leaders must analyse their behaviors and how they effect their companies as part of adaptive leadership training. HR can ensure that leaders learn from the past, adapt to the present, and prepare for the future by effectively transforming and demonstrating adaptive capacity. For the development of adaptive leadership a new leadership development framework is required. One that can be given at scale and creates adaptable leaders at all levels, sooner in their careers and in the flow of their work. The new model stresses learning in the context of the organisation's business conditions, processes, and objectives, as well as quick implementation of what has been learned. Starting with helping leaders understand the business, including its goals, mission, and goods and services, there are six activities and numerous keys to producing adaptable leaders.

Form an instructional design team made up of leaders from all levels and create a framework for discussion and creation of leadership training that senior leaders can utilize to ensure that everyone in the company understands what is essential to them and what is required of them. Give key objectives to the instructional design team that oversees human resources, corporate communications, employee relations, and other departments. This should be included in the whole employee experience, from recruiting to retirement.

Empower the instructional design team to lead corporate strategy, program management, operational excellence, and other teams in aligning target setting, investment portfolio management, and other goal-to-results approaches in order to maintain alignment as conditions change. Form an instructional design team made up of leaders from all levels and create a framework for discussion and creation of leadership training that senior leaders can utilise to ensure that everyone in the company understands what is essential to them and what is required of them.

Give key objectives to the instructional design team that oversees human resources, corporate communications, employee relations, and other departments. This should be included in the whole employee experience, from recruiting to retirement. Empower the instructional design team to lead corporate strategy, program management, operational excellence, and other teams in aligning target setting, investment portfolio management, and other goal-to-results approaches in order to maintain alignment as conditions change.

Employees have a say in where they work, shaping the dialogue, shaping the workplace, and eventually impacting leadership choices, which is a key part of adaptable workplaces. Employees' well-being, passion for the job, and dedication to the firm are all enhanced when they have a sense of choice and control over when, how, and where they conduct their work. Here are a few instances of workplaces that are adaptable: Siemens has stated that its workers would be able to work two or three days a week from wherever they feel most productive.

Employees at Twitter may work from anywhere in the world at any time. With no top-down-driven minimum need for in-office work, most professionals and project teams at Deloitte establish the adaptable working environment that works best for them and their clients.
Reports of reduced stress and burnout, as well as increased productivity and more time to focus on family support, as a result of the ability to telework or work remotely, even for one or two days per week. Using everyone's abilities rather

than simply those of top-level leaders is what an ideal talent mix includes.

A clear charter ensures that the organisation or team adheres to well-defined goals, responsibilities, and ground rules, while trust fosters strong links between workers, employers, and clients.Thoughts of transformation must begin inside the CLO, L & D, and other people management professionals if they are to effectively construct adaptable companies. Consider the following developing principles:

- To respond to opportunities and disruptions, cross-functional teams must adjust all organisational systems, including incentives and recognition, talent management, and learning and development.
- Start with your own internal knowledge and skills. When you've found adaptable leaders, search for leadership, technology, and management knowledge from outside sources to continue expanding your adaptive leadership schema.
- To help you scale, create a leadership team with a single leadership system attitude. Integrate organisational leadership competence and capacity into leaders' daily work flows.
- Incorporate critical thinking, diversity, and other behavioral competencies into the curriculum and learning environment.
- CLO and L & D professionals add value by empowering and mentoring organisation leaders at all levels, regardless of title or tenure.
- The C-suite adds value by keeping the company's strategy and goals up-to-date and clear. In this new model, CLOs and L & D professionals add value by empowering and mentoring organisational leaders at all

levels.

I would make it a point to focus on onboarding processes for new recruits, many of whom will work remotely due to spread teams and limited in-person connection chances. This entails establishing mentorship, shadowing, and relationship-building opportunities, as well as information transfer and training.

Virtual collaboration tools, shared documents, project-tracking tools, and knowledge libraries enable real-time transparency and documentation, ensuring that everyone in the team is up-to-date at all times.

> *"According to anecdotal evidence, virtual communication channels are especially effective with teenagers and young people."*

HR Analytics provides answers to crucial questions about the people who work for the company, allowing them to develop more robust systems for recruiting, productivity, pay, and retention. The following picture shows the essential questions.

- HR analytics benefits organisations by assisting them in making proactive decisions that help them mitigate risks and stay on top of things.
- It may assist in the provision of vital data and the subsequent improvement of spending, productivity, and operations, all of which benefit a business holistically.
- Reassuring staff that analytics enhances human decision-making, helps preserve rigor, and keeps initiatives focused on addressing business problems is one way organisations may overcome the hurdles of

embracing HR analytics.

- In the long run, the objective is to improve the HR function's analytical abilities and enable HR to better manage the workforce's future. This is the pressing need of the hour.

According to LinkedIn research, 93% of Indian organisations intend to fill available positions internally in the post-Covid era. Internal mobility, data-driven recruiting choices, and increasing employee experience are all emerging themes.

According to LinkedIn's Future of Talent research, in the post-covid age, more than 9 out of 10 (93%) Indian organisations are trying to fill available positions internally. The inaugural edition of the "Future of Talent" study, published by the professional networking platform, looked at the changing role of HR in India as well as how talent is acquired, engaged with, and developed in the current business climate. According to the research, companies are increasingly opting to fill positions internally.

The research also emphasises the rising emphasis on upskilling, which will be a key component of organisations' future workforce strategies. According to the research, 95% of Indian organisations have dedicated L & D programs to assist employees learn new skills and prepare for the future. Other developing trends, such as internal mobility, data-driven recruiting choices, and increasing employee experience, will be on businesses' minds in 2021.

According to the survey, 91% of Indian organisations utilise data to make educated talent-hiring decisions, and 53% use data to map capabilities to open job criteria. Furthermore, 9 out of 10 businesses are consolidating positions to save money on recruiting and make remote hiring more effective.

According to Gartner, organisations will continue to expand their use of contingent workers post-COVID-19 in order to maintain more flexibility in workforce management, and they will consider introducing other job models seen during the pandemic, such as talent sharing and 80% pay for 80% work.

According to McKinsey & Company, modest leaders exhibit "intentional calm," which helps them to disconnect from the circumstance and think more clearly about how to handle it. During times of transition, stability is both a struggle and a must.

Businesses need to offer even more security to employees and customers, who are already stressed by big lifestyle changes. This is best accomplished through a solid and resilient corporate culture, which may help organisations stay on track even when they embark on ambitious projects or face crises. The most successful organisations used a combination of proactive and reactive components to develop an agility-resilience framework, according to data collected from 325 enterprises. The study found that organisations with more agility-resilience had higher returns on investment and equity. As a result, more stability can aid adaptability and company survival during periods of rapid change.

An adaptive organisation is always better suited to meet difficulties and deal with adversity. People in such settings are more resilient and have a renewed willingness to face challenges. They are more capable of drifting through problems quickly as a consequence of their grit.

Accepting failure is the first step in becoming more adaptive. Accepting failure is not the same as giving up or quitting. Accepting setbacks as a transient situation is to invite failure. A stepping stone to knowledge. It's all about seizing opportunities to advance. Accepting different ideas from various people in business is one way to build a culture that is receptive to failure. Having a pulse on weather change energises consumers and provides incentives for trying out new products or services. It is critical for everyone to understand their role in delivering value to make a company adaptive.

Every member of the team is responsible for ensuring the organisation's success. Everyone must take the initiative and behave as a leader. Organisations must accept new ideas and make adjustments as a result. It is best to engage new minds and take advantage of their recent learning to ensure an influx of ideas. Employees must also be taught how to think and act strategically.

A mission that is obvious and unmistakable, presented as a simple "big concept" that all employees can connect to and are pleased to communicate with friends and coworkers. An atmosphere of shared responsibility for the organisation's future success, in which all employees are encouraged to think independently, be sensitive to one another, be kind and supportive of one another, and behave with humanity.

> *"Adaptability is essential for a company's ability to respond successfully to changing business conditions."*

Almost every company prepares how to function when business conditions are predictable, but the key to long-term survival is being able to adapt successfully to the unexpected. The mission statement is important because it informs you what to focus on and what to focus on doing.

It is simply the measures you take on a regular basis to achieve your objective.

As a result, vision and mission must be in sync. Missions, like visions, should be clear, succinct, and easy to understand. After all, they are guidelines on how everyone in the company should focus their efforts. Surprisingly, the study of business objectives is hampered by a lack of unanimity and clarity about what constitutes a strong purpose.

As an adaptable leader, you must assist all members of your business in identifying the fundamental mission guidelines that collectively lead to the vision you all desire. A mission must be quantifiable as well. This is necessary so that leadership can regularly analyse the extent to which your mission's work activities are contributing to the achievement of your vision.

Furthermore, good missions do not exist in frames and webpages. They exist in the hearts and minds of everyone in your organisation. How probable is it that if you strolled around your building and randomly questioned 10 workers from different levels of your business, they would be able to recite and describe your purpose without having to look it up? If they are unable to describe your mission, you don't have one.

High-performance businesses are adaptable, sensing market shifts and making strategic adjustments on the fly. The broad strokes of traditional strategy are supplemented rather than replaced by this approach. They provide their organisations' peripheries—far from the traditional strategy function—the authority to act in response to market changes.

Furthermore, successful companies regularly monitor and measure their adherence to these traits with the same zeal and expertise they demand of themselves in terms of financial and operational performance.

"The search for the optimal organisational and human traits is no longer a black box."

The idea is that the organisation would reach peak performance through improving the psychological well-being of its employees. As a result, the culture must contain triggers that cause people to act in specific ways and feel accountable for the company's future success. Purpose, vision, cultural values, business values, and architecture are the key causes.

The ability to constantly analyse all relevant information in order to adjust to current impacts is critical for business agility. If not, can you make them more relevant by transforming them? All too frequently, executives devote valuable effort to developing risk management and business continuity strategies only to realise that their organisations are unprepared to deal with an environment that is more volatile and uncertain than ever before.

"Organisational resilience—an organisation's capacity to foresee, plan for, respond to, and adapt to gradual change and unexpected shocks in order to survive and thrive—is the answer."

Resilience is a long-term and often insurmountable problem. Organisations in every industry are continuously tested and stretched by slow-growing disruptions as well as shocks and disasters. The repercussions of operational failures in a more connected society have been highlighted by recent high-profile blunders, accidents, and tragedies. Organisations sleepwalk into failure due to complex and sometimes unnoticed systemic organisational flaws and cultural difficulties.

The creation of answers to these resilience issues is as much a leadership and organisational challenge as it is a scientific and technological undertaking. In many respects, the adaptability required over a longer period of time as the context, product or service needs in the industry change is even more challenging.

Following the status quo, which has worked successfully in the past, may result in success progressively fading when new businesses emerge with new operational models or services. This sort of adjustment requirement might be subtle, only becoming obvious when it is too late.

Organisations must be receptive to the idea of future-proofing their processes and products. organisational resilience entails not just avoiding or responding to negative occurrences, but also 'shifting before the cost of not changing becomes too high,' utilising opportunities, and pushing innovation in order to be competitive in the face of adversity.

Organisations must be receptive to the idea of future-proofing their processes and products. organisational resilience entails not just avoiding or responding to negative occurrences, but also 'shifting before the cost of not changing becomes too high,' utilising opportunities, and pushing innovation in order to be competitive in the face of adversity. It's not always easy to see the broad picture, handle change, and succeed without stumbling over what's directly in front of you.

In the long run, an adaptive lens may be more successful in solving this problem. If you think this is an adaptive difficulty, you should spend some time investigating what's going on. You might enlist the help of your HR department or engage an outside expert to do an objective evaluation of what is pushing your staff to go. It's possible that the issue isn't with the wage structure or the incentive system, but with the overall culture of the company. In most teams, there is a general lack of responsibility, and employees blame one another for not meeting deliverables. Further investigation may reveal that the organisation's leadership team, which includes you, is just as much a part of the equation as you are.

High-performance companies have clearly defined responsibilities that are meticulously put together to make a highly efficient company. People are aware of what is expected of them and which decisions they have control over. Employees understand when and with whom they must cooperate when accountability is shared. Role charters are one way we help organisations achieve this clarity, but the name is less essential than having a route to explicit accountability, decision rights, and behavioral requirements. Clear roles eliminate the uncertainty that hinders decision-making and boost modern businesses' performance potential and employee engagement. Peers in a company can use role charters to have open and honest discussions about individual, collective, and shared responsibilities.

"The dawn of our emerging future, wherein the perceptions and practises of yesterday melt amid the heat of the moment, alchemically reconfiguring new pathways, perspectives, principles, and behaviours, contrasts sharply with the outdated yet still prevalent logic of yesterday with its hallmark models, mindsets, and metrics."- Dr. Amit Das

While many businesses excel in recruitment, training, or performance management, high-performance organisations excel at translating their company plan into a compelling people strategy. HR serves as a key advisor to business units on both operational and strategic people concerns in these businesses. It includes short- and long-term strategies for attracting, developing, and keeping the best individuals with the best skills.

Employer brands are well-defined in high-performance organisations. Employees and recruits alike are aware of the wide variety of perks available to them, including professional growth, job rotation, and prestige, as well as flexibility and autonomy. This brand—or employee value proposition—contributes to a company's competitive advantage and strengths.

Employee development is prioritised in high-performance organisations, which invest in training and rotation of jobs and responsibilities. These encounters may beat remuneration and other financial incentives as a significant motivator and retention strategy. They also promote teamwork and decrease the chances of localised leadership. By the time they reach the upper echelons, employees have a comprehensive view of the company.

Talent management is a far larger function than most businesses believe. It isn't just for those who are on the fast track. It also addresses the people and jobs that are crucial to a company's success. The management of bad performers is the polar opposite of talent management. The way a company manages the development or departure of low-performing individuals sends a strong message to the rest of the company about what will be tolerated and praised. HR is a strategic partner and a business enabler. People strategy is as important as business strategy in leading organisations.

However, you must consider the nature of the task you are confronted with. Adaptive organisations, according to Deloitte, will succeed. To become an adaptable organisation, large-scale global enterprises must make a fundamental shift in operating and management philosophy that allows them to function with a start-up mindset and drive current people practices that enable enterprise agility through an empowered network of teams. The findings of recent survey demonstrate that organisational speed is a critical component of outperformance in times of extraordinary change, and they suggest three approaches for firms to increase speed in the long run.

Organisations should assess the relationship between their mission and how it is carried out on a daily basis. More clarity about why the organisation exists should serve as a north star for crucial business decisions, including capital allocation, employee experience, and workforce choices recruiting, reskilling, upskilling programs. Organisations that make a clear connection between what they do and why they exist are more likely to retain employees and customers.

"The dawn of our emerging future, wherein the perceptions and practises of yesterday melt amid the heat of the moment, alchemically reconfiguring new pathways, perspectives, principles, and behaviours, contrasts sharply with the outdated yet still prevalent logic of yesterday with its hallmark models, mindsets, and metrics."

- Dr. Amit Das

References

- *Leadership 2050: Critical Challenges, Key Contexts and Emerging Trends (Building Leadership Bridges) Paperback – July 24, 2015 by Matthew Sowcik (Author).*
- *2030: How Today's Biggest Trends Will Collide and Reshape the Future of Everything Hardcover – 25 August 2020 by Mauro F. Guillen (Author).*
- *Future Fit: How to Stay Relevant and Competitive in the Future of Work Paperback – Import, 25 May 2021 by Andrea Clarke (Author).*
- *Made in Future: A Story of Marketing, Media, and Content for our Times Hardcover – Import, 16 May 2022 by Prashant Kumar (Author).*
- *The Future Is Faster Than You Think Paperback – 17 February 2020 by Peter H. Diamandis and Steven Kotler (Author).*
- *Leadership: Theory and practice. Los Angeles, CA: SAGE Publications, Inc by Northouse, P. published 2019.*
- *All Systems Go: The Change Imperative for Whole System Reform (Paperback)by Michael Fullan, published 2010.*
- *The Constructivist Leader (Paperback) by Deborah Walker,published 1995.*
- *Credibility: How Leaders Gain and Lose It, Why People Demand It (Paperback) by James M. Kouzes, published 1993.*
- *Appreciative Leadership: Focus on What Works to Drive Winning Performance and Build a Thriving Organization (Hardcover) by Diana Whitney, published 2010.*
- *Thinking, Fast and Slow (Hardcover) by Daniel Kahneman, published 2011.*

REFERENCES

- *The Checklist Manifesto: How to Get Things Right (Hardcover)* by Atul Gawande, published 2009.
- *The Heart of Change: Real-Life Stories of How People Change Their Organizations (Hardcover)* by John P. Kotter (Goodreads Author), published 2002.
- *Harvard Business Review on Leading Through Change (Paperback)* by Harvard Business School Press (Compilation), published 2006.
- *Boards That Lead: When to Take Charge, When to Partner, and When to Stay Out of the Way (Hardcover)* by Ram Charan, published 2013.
- *Innovation in the Schoolhouse: Entrepreneurial Leadership in Education (ebook)by Jack Leonard, published 2013.*
- *Chaos, Complexity and Leadership 2012 (Hardcover)* by Santo Banerjee (Editor), published 2013.
- *Checklist for Change: Making American Higher Education a Sustainable Enterprise (Hardcover)by Robert Zemsky, published 2013.*
- *Nudge: Improving Decisions About Health, Wealth, and Happiness (Paperback)* by Richard H. Thaler, published 2008.
- *Leverage Leadership: A Practical Guide to Building Exceptional Schools (Paperback)* by Doug Lemov, published 2012.
- *Rethinking Leadership: A Collection of Articles (Paperback)* by Thomas J. Sergiovanni (Editor), published 1999.
- *Leadership on the Line, With a New Preface: Staying Alive Through the Dangers of Change (Kindle Edition)* by Ronald A. Heifetz.
- *We Want to Do More Than Survive: Abolitionist Teaching and the Pursuit of Educational Freedom (Hardcover)* by Bettina L. Love, published 2019.

REFERENCES

- *The Leadership Gap, What Gets Between You and Your Greatness by Lolly Daskal, published 2017.*
- *The Power of Positive Leadership, How and Why Positive Leaders Transform Teams and Organizations and Change the World by Jon Gordon, published 2017.*
- *Wooden on Leadership, How to Create a Winning Organization by John Wooden, Steve Jamison, published 2005.*
- *Learning Leadership, The Five Fundamentals of Becoming an Exemplary Leader by James M. Kouzes, Barry Z. Posner, published 2016.*
- *5 Levels of Leadership, Proven Steps to Maximize Your Potential by John C. Maxwell, published 2013.*
- *Real Leadership, 9 Simple Practices for Leading and Living with Purpose by John Addison, John David Mann, published in 2016.*
- *TouchPoints, Creating Powerful Leadership Connections in the Smallest of Moments by Douglas Conant, Mette Norgaard, published 2011.*
- *Organizational Culture and Leadership by Edgar H. Schein, published 2010.*
- *The Practice of Adaptive Leadership, Tools and Tactics for Changing Your Organization and the World by Ronald A. Heifetz, Marty Linsky, Alexander Grashow, published 2009.*
- *Reinventing the Organization: How Companies Can Deliver Radically Greater Value in Fast-Changing Markets by Arthur Yeung & Dave Ulrich, Sept 2019.*
- *Organizational Theory, Design and Change | Seventh Edition | By Pearson Paperback – 26 December 2017 by R Jones Gareth (Author), Matthew Mary (Author).*

About The Author

Dr. Amit Das, is a renowned executive advisor, consultant, educationist, author, speaker, counsellor, and coach whose 25+ years of business experience provides high-impact, practical solutions that support his clients' leadership development and organisational transformations. He worked for three great fortune 500 MNCs and left rich leagacy of organising transformational learning workshops. He has transformed more than 5000+ working executives through his path breaking soft skills training workshops. Dr. Amit Das is recognised as an innovative, principled thought leader who combines intellectual rigor and discipline with an ability to translate theory into practice. His operational skills are coupled with a strategic ability to analyse, develop, and implement successful strategies for profitability, growth, and sustainability.

Dr. Amit Das has a successful track record in aligning learning and training solutions to key business strategy with a strong focus on flawless execution excellence to facilitate individual, business divisional, and organisational performance. He keeps relentless focus on measuring training impact and ROI, people capability building graphs, training process governance, performance coaching, and strategic thinking. These have been some of his key individual success traits. His core capabilities include performance coaching, designing training and development frameworks, psychometric assessment and analysis, competency framework development and assessments, content design and facilitation of soft skills and leadership programmes, Learning Management Systems, Learning Impact Measurement, Talent Analysis, and Performance Coaching and Counselling.

ABOUT THE AUTHOR

Dr. Amit Das has authored multiple management and self-development books, like Create Your Leadership Edge, Building Organisational Capability, Ethical Road Map, Attomic Attention, BYPB, Implementor, ALOUD, Redefining Talent Management, Defining Your Success Factors, Lead or Plead, Make The Most Of Your Life, Better Half or Bitter Half, Organisational Transformation Through Learning, The Transformative Mind & Soul are few of them.

He has a Ph.D. and a Fellowship in strategic learning, along with his first class degrees in Human Resource Management, Marketing Management, International Business, and Corporate Laws from the top business schools in India. He is a certified Psychometric analyst, HR Metrics, OD Interventionist, Human Psychologist, Lifecoach, Leadership Developer, Black Belt (LSS), Strategic Thinker, Talent Analyst, certified professional trainer from the U.K. and certified behavioral coach from the U.S.A.

Dr. Amit Das likes googling, reading books, writing articles & books, cooking, listening to old melodies, and counselling people to unleash their true potential to build a strong nation. He is married and blessed with a son. He would love to hear about your experience after reading his books. You can email him and share your thoughts, or you can use his services for life coaching, positive behavioural counseling, educational support, and mentoring for young, promising students pursuing their B.B.A. and M.B.A. degrees.